PRAISE FOR
CONFESSIONS OF A WORRYWART

"A first-rate personal essayist, Susan Orlins delivers the goods time and again. Underneath her self-mocking voice, her abundant humor, her brio, there is the serious candor of a moralist who worries the problems that won't go away."

—PHILLIP LOPATE, author and editor of
The Art of the Personal Essay

"Susan Orlins is America's funniest neurotic since Woody Allen. Just be careful you don't crack a rib reading *Confessions of a Worrywart.*"

—PATRICIA VOLK, author of *Stuffed*

"Susan Orlins combines the practical with the comical. A multi-tasking mom, she knows how to show and hide her feelings simultaneously. When you have the time (the kids are out of the house and your mom is in a home), read this book! You will identify and laugh."

—SYBIL SAGE, writer for *The Mary Tyler Moore Show, Growing Pains, Magnum P.I., Northern Exposure*

"Toxic chemicals. Tomatoes. Getting the bed by the window in her future nursing home. What's NOT to worry about? Just ask Susan Orlins, America's funniest worrywart—not because you want to wring your hands, but because you want to laugh out loud. Her offbeat take on all challenges, great and small, is a delight."

— DIANE MACEACHERN, author of *Big Green Purse*

About The Author

Susan Orlins began chronicling her worries in 2009 on her blog, *Confessions of a Worrywart*. She also contributes to *Huffington Post* and writes about food, relationships, travel, and more on NBC Universal's *Life Goes Strong* website.

Orlins has published in *The New York Times*, *Newsday*, *The Pennsylvania Gazette*, and *The Washington Post Magazine*. For several years, she was a contributing editor at *Moment Magazine*, where she received a Rockower Award for her profile of socio-linguist Deborah Tannen.

After adopting an infant in China in 1986, Orlins wrote a letter home that appears in *Women's Letters: from the Revolutionary War to the Present*. *Chicken Soup for the Soul* published her essay "Marathon Women" in *Like Mother, Like Daughter: Our 101 Best Stories*.

Orlins is the divorced mother of three daughters in their twenties and thirties, who are what she worries about most. She leads a nonfiction workshop for homeless people in Washington, D.C., where she lives with her aging pound hound, Casey, about whom she also worries.

To Barbara

Oy!

CONFESSIONS *of a* WORRYWART

HUSBANDS, LOVERS, MOTHERS, AND OTHERS

Susan Orlins

SENECA BOOKS

Portions of this work previously appeared in the following: *The Washington Post Magazine*, *Women's Letters: from the Revolutionary War to the Present*, *The Pennsylvania Gazette*, and on the websites *Huffington Post* and *Confessions of a Worrywart*.

ISBN:0615600018
ISBN-13:978-0615600017

Cover design by Rodrigo Corral Design
Illustration by Mark Stutzman
Interior design by Kim Sillen Gledhill

Printed in the United States of America

For my daughters Eliza, Sabrina, and Emily
as well as my beagle, Casey, who has been balled up beside me during
practically every keystroke.

And to the memory of my mom, Millie Fishman,
and my dad, Matt Fishman.

CONTENTS

INTRODUCTION

BOYFRIENDS AND SUCH

ROUND EYE IN CHINA

MARRIED WITH KIDS

DIVORCED WITH KIDS

DIVORCED WITH DOG

So Long, Mom

Searching For Susan Fishman

Postscript

Guide For Further Discussion 279

Acknowledgments 282

INTRODUCTION

Worrying about
Writing about Worrying
2012

Sometimes I play a game in which I name an object and then associate a worry with it, just to see if I can stump myself.

"Venetian blinds," I say.

"Peeping Tom!" I answer without having inhaled.

"Tomatoes," I try. "Salmonella poisoning!"

Another way to play is to see how many worries I can associate with a single object. For instance, I could add choking on a sandwich to the tomato category. I simply cannot draw a blank in the association game; there is no end to all that can go wrong. So imagine how much setting out to write a book aroused in me a sense of danger.

Yet I am not without my optimistic stripe. I can envision an outcome in which spilling my anxieties onto the page results in a transfusion for my mind, ridding me of the very fears I write about, thus allowing mental space for imaginings of, say, joyful days in the nursing home sometime in the distant future.

Ah, the nursing home. I'm still trying to decide whether the company of a roommate—if there's a choice—will be worth the risk of being around someone who might, for example, deposit fingernail clippings on the night table between our beds. My three twenty-something daughters already know that if I do land in a shared room, they should claim for me the bed by the window. And, in case I can't speak for myself, I have asked them repeatedly to arrange for the window to be open whenever possible, though not when someone outside is operating a leaf blower.

Speaking of my daughters, I, of the association game described above, am reminded of another problem with airing my worries publicly. Although presently there are no marriages for my girls on the horizon, let's say they get married one day. What if my new in-laws happen upon my confessions? Will they think I'm a screwball? (Really, Future In-Laws, I'm not as dotty as I may seem.)

The same problem could arise if I were to meet Mr. Right, or for that matter, Mr. Wrong. (I spent a very enjoyable four years with a Mr. Wrong, so I'm not at all opposed to getting another one.) If such a Mister were to read my ruminations on loathsome scenarios, it might put the kibosh on our relationship just as it's getting started.

Thinking about my future in-laws makes me wonder how we'll divide visits with our children. And grandchildren! Will it lead to competitive Thanksgivings? I'm divorced and let's say all my theoretical future sons-in-laws' parents are divorced. Then what? Will we have to divide holidays eight ways?

So you see, my worries cast a broad net, covering everything from my dog's self-esteem to decapitation by ceiling fan. My anxiety also extends to the complicated territory of relationships: with my mother, daughters, ex-husbands, boyfriends, and therapists, who are like boyfriends, but who can't dump me.

With all these worries, I am fearful I'll appear frivolous or insensitive, especially to those with real problems. My cousin, whose daughter has cystic fibrosis, once told me, "When they find a cure for C.F., I'll worry about world peace."

In 2003, shortly after a 200-year-old poplar tree fell on my house, causing damage that took a year to repair, I said to my psychiatrist, "How can I complain, given that we're safe, while my friend's son just died in a car crash?"

He responded with the shrink party line, "You're entitled to your worries." Entitled? Perhaps. But who can deny that there is a hierarchy of worry-worthiness?

I can't recall a time I did not think like a worrywart. As Queen Isabella in the third grade play, the only way I could keep from giggling was to conjure up an image of my mother dying (she lived to be ninety-two).

During my own years of young, plump motherhood, while writing a diet tips article, I lost twelve pounds. Now, by examining my imagined sequences of fearsome events, maybe I will indeed shed some worry weight.

I have changed some names and minor details. Otherwise, I have written these stories the way I remember them.

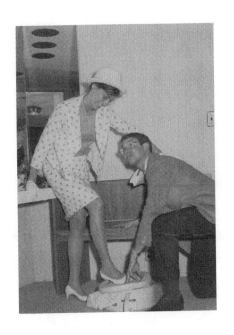

BOYFRIENDS
AND SUCH

PUSH PULL
1950

Howard Goldman was my first crush. He had curly hair and a freckly look, but what attracted me to him was a small scar, the shape of a crescent moon, smack between his eyebrows. At the end of each kindergarten day we faced each other, feet planted firmly apart, hands pressed palm-to-palm. Then we pushed, grunting and grimacing, a tug-of-war in reverse. No matter how clenched our teeth or how reddened our faces, neither of us ever budged the other, as in a perfectly-matched arm wrestling contest. So began for me the business of pushing boys away when I wanted them to stay and getting pushed in return, the offense and defense not readily distinguishable.

If one of us was holding back, it was not I; the opportunity to take on the opposite sex in any form of battle charged me with resolve. And whenever I succeeded in demonstrating a boy's inferiority, my nostrils flared with satisfaction.

Maybe my obsession to outwit, out-push, or out-anything else a boy was because of the hundred times my mother had told me, "Daddy almost fell off his chair when he found out you were a girl." The logic was there for him: he already had a daughter, he wanted a son, and he always believed the next card dealt him would be a trump. If a downpour eased for a nanosecond, Daddy would say, "Look! It's clearing up. It's gonna be a beeoo-tee-ful day." My parents were different that way. Once, on a honeysuckle-sweet afternoon, I saw a cloud float between my mother and the sun, casting a momentary shadow. She hastily gathered herself up, warning everyone within earshot, "Oy, it's gonna rain." Like my mother, I was a worrywart; like my father, I searched under every shadow for the sun rays.

IMPERFECTIONS
1952

What was it about imperfections that attracted me? Boys with scars and crooked teeth had a vulnerable look that those with smooth skin and uniform teeth did not. Michael Ellis had two different eyebrows: one came to a point in the middle like a circumflex. He was in third grade, I was in second. So practically the only time I got to admire his pale, slight figure was on the school bus. While singing "God of our Fathers" in assembly, I would get a romantic feeling just knowing he was in the auditorium.

Sometimes I awoke in the night with an ache thinking about him. Once, I shuffled to my mother's bedside for comfort. "Mommy, I can't sleep. I keep thinking about Michael Ellis." The hollowest part of night was the only time I didn't feel too ashamed to utter a boy's name in my house, because it was the only time there was no risk of being teased about liking someone by my older sister, Ellen, and my younger brother, Mark.

"Oy, Susie, Susie. Go back to sleep. Close your eyes and picture a meadow of lollipop trees." That was her antidote for unrequited love? Lollipops may have worked for bad dreams. But now whenever I closed my eyes, it was as if a picture of the pert little face of Michael Ellis was glued inside my lids. I repeated his name, rolling on my tongue all those Ls until daybreak.

Once during a fire drill, while waiting in the schoolyard, I got close enough to notice he had clumps of wax in his ears. In that instant, all ardor for him drained from my body; I never thought about him again. The experience taught me nothing.

RICKY NELSON AND ME
1958

In seventh grade my girlfriends and I were not part of the popular crowd of girls who looked sexy in gym suits and paired off with boys. Instead, we immersed ourselves in a world of make-believe.

We were three couples: me and Ricky Nelson, Phyllis Kirschner and Tab Hunter, Shessie Einbinder and Pat Boone. Each "family" had one child as well as a fat scrapbook filled with photos of the husband and gossipy headlines cut from movie magazines. On the wall next to my bed I taped a picture of Ricky wearing a cowboy suit with pants so tight you could see a bulge in his crotch.

On TV, I saw other star-struck girls scream when they watched Ricky perform. Then one sultry afternoon I squeezed in among thousands of sweating, lovesick teenagers at Steel Pier in Atlantic City to see his show. Once the shrieking started, I joined in and couldn't stop; each time I screamed louder than the time before until I thought the veins in my neck would pop.

Nearly two decades later I was living in D.C., where Ricky was featured at The Cellar Door, a small nightclub in Georgetown. Only now he was called Rick. To prove that childhood dreams could come true, I decided to go say hello. The club owner, a friend of mine, helped me time my arrival between the seven-thirty and nine-thirty shows.

Still in a tennis skirt from a game I had played earlier, I dashed in and said, "I wanted to meet you in order to prove that childhood dreams can come true."

"Thanks," said Rick. "Are you staying for the show?"

God, it had never occurred to me to stay for the show; I had moved on. "Gee, I'm sorry I can't," I answered and hurried away.

I still can't believe he's dead.

FIRST KISS
1959

I met Ronnie Pinsker at a Pokerino arcade on what my girlfriend Jeanie and I called slut night. Earlier that day, my mother had dropped Jeanie and me off in downtown Philly, where we had boarded a bus to Atlantic City to spend the weekend at my grandparents' small apartment two blocks from the beach. As soon as we arrived, we changed into shorts and halter tops and set out to prowl the boardwalk and look at boys.

I hadn't considered actually *meeting* a boy but, while Jeanie was puckering at her image in the tiny mirror of a four-for-a-quarter photo machine and applying Oh-So-Pink to her lips, a boy came up to me and said, "Hi. I'm Ronnie."

After establishing that we both lived in Philly, he asked, "What are you doing next Saturday?"

"I don't know. I'll be here, I guess." I hated how stupid I sounded.

"Do you want to go to the movies?" he asked.

"Okay," I answered, trying to sound nonchalant. Clumsily, I dug in my pocketbook and found a pencil with which I wrote my grandparents' phone number on the back of a Skee-Ball coupon.

All week I could think of nothing else, partly because I was ecstatic and partly because I was scared to death, since he was only the second boy who had ever asked me out. The first boy had been Lionel Kolker from my class; I was so embarrassed to have gone on a date with him that, afterwards, I never spoke to him again.

Ronnie picked me up in his two-tone pink and white Ford. After we watched a movie that I couldn't follow and ate hamburgers with the works, he drove for several blocks, then parked on one of those streets whose names you find on a Monopoly board.

"Lavender Blue" played on the car radio. Ronnie was sixteen, I was thirteen, and my grandparents were eighty-five and, no doubt, waiting up for me. Ronnie put his right arm around my shoulder and with his left index finger on my chin, he turned my face to his. Then he attached his mouth to mine—open!

I wasn't ready for this. Married couples on TV didn't even sleep in the same bed. I honestly never imagined what kissing a boy would be like. The closest I had ever come to a real kiss was in sixth grade when Jeanie and I would pretend to make out, using one of our hands as a partition between her lips and mine. But our mouths were never open. I felt like a fish being deprived of oxygen. My left arm, squashed under the weight of his body, tingled with pins and needles, but I didn't dare move for fear my stomach would gurgle. When at last it was over and I could inhale again, I noticed that Ronnie's face smelled like onions and ketchup and popcorn butter. On the ride back to my grandparents' apartment, I wondered if my face smelled as awful as his.

The following week, back in Philadelphia, my girlfriend Bev said you could get pregnant from that kind of kissing, which I knew was not true. Then I received my first love letter. "As I look towards the endless sky there is a star missing. I know who took it and who will bring it back." I must have read Ronnie's letter three thousand times, but I saw him only three more times, including our last date in Philly, when he brought me a carton filled with wheels of grosgrain ribbon—yellows, greens, purples, wide ones, narrow ones—from his father's ribbon factory.

Over more than half a century, those ribbons have moved with me to more than a dozen different homes. I have consumed them bit by bit, as though by winding them around my daughters' pony tails and birthday packages, I have been weaving my life in, out, and around until one day I'll reach the ends of those ribbon rolls and then I'll die.

THE CRUSH LIST
1961

Everything in my life was motivated by a crush or the quest for one. Tuesday mornings, during tenth-grade study hall, my friend Bobbi and I would make our crush lists for the week. A boy could qualify with things like a Band-Aid placed at an alluring angle across his knuckle, in which case we labeled him a Band-Aid crush. Characters from our history books, such as Woodrow Wilson or Clarence Darrow, could make the lists too. If a boy was good-looking but we weren't attracted to him, he landed in the anti-crush category. My chipped tooth crushes were so numerous that I gave them their own separate page.

THE ONE I NEVER FORGOT
1962

I never took books home from high school. I did math homework in French and French homework in math. Those subjects were easy. History was harder.

Luke Landau had Mr. Ashcom first period for history, and I had the same class after lunch. Ashcom always reviewed a test with us immediately after he gave it and, as though setting a trap for cheaters, he gave the same questions to each class. For a quiz on the Revolutionary War, Luke had written the correct responses on the back of a Doublemint gum wrapper, which he handed to me in the cafeteria. I quickly memorized them.

During the first five minutes of taking the test, I whizzed through twenty-five of the twenty-six matching questions. Then I felt Ashcom peering over my shoulder. Realizing the folly of finishing so quickly, I made the last answer wrong, imagining I could trick him into thinking I hadn't cheated after all. Weird Ashcom drew a line through all the correct matches, and then encircled the single wrong one. He gave me credit for only that one and said, "Please come see me at the end of the day."

Later that afternoon, as I entered his classroom, Ashcom peered at me through his Benjamin Franklin spectacles and said, "Tell me who gave you the answers."

"I can't," I replied.

"Well," he said, "you can do it here now or later in the principal's office in a flood of tears with your parents present."

It never occurred to me to refuse both alternatives; I knew I would capitulate. But I could not make Luke's name come out of my mouth. So Ashcom handed me a pencil and told me to point to it on a class list. Although Luke did not hold it against me, I felt like I owed him something I could not repay.

Luke and I had always been friends. Then, in the middle of eleventh grade his mother died from stomach cancer. The second I heard was the exact moment I became attracted to him. It was as if, on the day she died, the love floated out of her body and lodged itself in mine.

A small calendar stood on Luke's desk. On January 5 he had written: *Mother died 9:30 p.m.* The February 8 entry read: *I love Sue F.*

Tall and lanky, Luke had yellow-flecked eyes that could burn a hole right through a girl's heart. He had a scar on his left nostril and his two front teeth overlapped. One tooth had a chip. His hands were the hands of a carpenter, large and strong with prominent veins. The Wrangler jeans he wore hung low on his hips and fit so snugly I used to joke that they were biting him. His button-down shirts were crisply ironed and the shine on his brown penny loafers could have passed an army inspection. It was not clear what, if anything, his father did—

the family never seemed to have much money—yet they wore Brooks Brothers clothes and they drove a Porsche.

Luke got mostly Cs in school, but he knew how to make jewelry, build furniture, and catch fish, skills that—to me—transcended grades. He could be sweet, occasionally, like the time he came over and said he had a present for me that began with the letter O. I ran with him to his car, certain it was a floating opal, but it turned out to be a Ouija board. Since the guiding forces in my life were horoscopes and Chinese cookie fortunes, I was delighted by the expanded possibilities the Ouija offered.

There was another gift. One night we were in HoJo's sipping milkshakes with a bunch of friends. Luke got up to go to the bathroom, and when he returned, he tossed a small blue box in my lap. I opened it. Inside, a diamond ring was winking at me. I gasped so loud that the entire restaurant became silent. For that one moment I had the queerest feeling that Luke wanted to marry me and that, yes, this would be it; I accepted that the rest of my life could fit inside this tiny blue box. At the same time, awareness floated across my mind that girls like me, who lived in split-level homes and earned high math scores, did not get married in high school. All those thoughts occurred in the few seconds before I realized that Luke had gotten the ring by depositing a quarter or two into a vending machine in the men's room.

Whenever my mother let me drive her purple Oldsmobile after school, I would put the top down and head to Luke's neighborhood. I never understood why, as strict as my father was, he allowed me to drive, given that the township police had phoned our house numerous times to report sightings of me doing eighty on the winding back roads.

When cruising past Luke's house, however, I would lighten up on the gas pedal, then double back, eyes straight ahead, trying not to look obvious. Sometimes he would notice me passing by and shout for me to come in.

Up in his room we would lie on the bed with my nose burrowed into his neck, which smelled like a starched shirt, even when he wasn't wearing a shirt. Soon the touching would begin. If he reached to unhook my bra, I would push his hand away. Then it would spring back and I'd push it away again. Depending on the amount of pressure I applied, he would know whether it was the no that meant no or the no that meant yes.

Did we ever talk about anything more than high school gossip? I can't remember a single conversation. I simply craved Luke in direct proportion to how much he taunted me by flirting with other girls. And, of course, I went out of my way to dish it back. The ongoing drama between us sustained our passion at a feverish peak.

Luke inflicted the deepest wounds when he pursued my biggest girl crush, Nancy Ernst, a cheerleader with large, liquid-blue eyes and wispy, blonde bangs. My friend Ginger would retrieve from the trash the notes Luke and Nancy had passed during English class. It killed me to read their correspondences, yet I read them over and over. (Does everyone hold onto this kind of thing in a small wooden box for fifty years?)

Nancy: *I heard you told some guy that you got me! Thanks a lot!*

Luke: *I might have said I'd love to get you but I never said I did! But now I don't want to because we've spoiled it—we asked.*

Nancy: *If you are semi-back with Sue, are we still going out? Does she still hate me?*

Luke: *I figured that you were going to break the date so I booked up the weekend with Sue. If you want to go out Friday tell me. I'll break the date with her. It won't be one of your wild weekends. It will be a nice quiet one with music and a bottle. (alone!)*

Nancy: *That's okay, but what does she have to say—doesn't she care?*

Luke: *Look I've taken about enough of Sue's noise. I'll admit I like her but I want to go out with you and even if she cares it will make no difference. If she trusts me she won't care.*

I kept the crumpled pages in a box under my bed. (And, yes, fifty years later they remain in that box.) Was Luke so dim that he didn't get the contradiction in his comment about my trusting him while he was putting the moves on Nancy? The more I read the notes, the more determined I was to fight back. Whenever Luke saw me sashay up to another boy, he'd corner me at the end of the day and slam me against my locker. Then I would have to make excuses for the black and blue marks on my arm to my mother, who seemed torn between her maternal instinct toward the motherless Luke and her instinct to protect her daughter from one she suspected to be trouble.

Throughout the rest of high school, we regularly broke up and then made up. During one of our breakups, the summer after graduation, a boy named Saul asked me out. A couple of years later, Saul and I married, but I never forgot Luke.

When he was in his mid-twenties, Luke married a woman who was forty-five, his mother's age when she died.

Sometimes I take a train that passes through Philadelphia;

just before pulling into 30th Street Station, I check my hair in the window glass. Then I search the platform for his face. Every ten years when we have a high school reunion, I ask my old friend Brenda, who is still the class organizer, "Will Luke be coming?"

Brenda calls to ask him. He always says no and then asks, "How's Sue?"

STARTER MARRIAGE
1963–1965

One of my least evolved relationships was with Saul, my first husband. His dimpled cheeks and large, almost bulging eyes gave him a perky Jiminy Cricket look. He also looked like Frank Sinatra, though Saul wore glasses with pink-hued, transparent frames. His mother claimed his I.Q. was at the genius level. My mother thought he was nice.

On our first date, four days before I entered the University of Pennsylvania, Saul and I made out in an overgrown meadow where I contracted poison ivy so severe that blisters as big as balloons erupted on my knees and elbows. "Where did you pick this up, Susie?" my mother asked in a tone suggesting I had acquired it voluntarily, the way she "picked up" my father's shirts at the Chinese laundry.

Although I considered myself an adept liar, my voice shot up uncommonly high. "How should I know?" I fixed my eyes on the spool of gauze she was unraveling. Having to bear up under my mother's glare and also resemble a mummy for my first day of college was a fair exchange for that breathless romp in the cool evening grass.

Saul, a senior pre-med student, lived a two-hour drive from my dorm in West Philadelphia. Autumn weekends I huddled beside him over textbooks at a bridge table in his parents' backyard, in the same Philadelphia suburb where my parents lived, studying with the intensity of a Talmudic scholar; had he been a Hell's Angel, I would have clung to his midriff from the rear of a Harley.

After a dozen reruns of the same week, I began to weary of the monthly anniversary celebrations of our first date and the perfunctory "I love you" that punctuated the end of every phone call. Like too many lumps of cookie dough crowded onto a baking sheet in a hot oven, our core ingredients were fusing into a single mass. I seduced myself into believing it was amusing to shuttle with him from one coffee house to another, mutely sipping ginger ale while Oscar Brand or some other pale guitarist I'd never heard of led the audience in folksy sing-alongs. At the clap-along parts, my palms would meet on the off beats. As hard as I tried to tailor myself to this new life, it didn't quite fit, the same way my mother's dresses, safety-pinned at the waist, never hung just so over my narrow hips.

My true impulses nipped at the borders of my consciousness. I wanted to sizzle with passion, scream at someone and with someone, scare myself to death drag racing or skydiving, quit college. I had to swat away memories that buzzed in my head, like flies on a window, of frenzied fighting and lusty make-up sessions only months earlier with Luke of the slender Wranglers and keen eye for the girls.

Even a smidge of the quarreling and making up I'd had

with bad-boy Luke would have helped to quiet my adrenaline cravings. Sharing tender whispers with Saul in his madras shirt and khakis, his dimpled grin and parallel teeth that twinkled like bathroom tile made me feel like a fraud. Although the whole thing didn't feel right, it didn't feel altogether wrong. I did not give much thought to what attracted me to Saul, just as I had never given much thought to anything other than having fun and attracting boys.

Saul was different from other boyfriends I'd had, husband material (not that I was at all, in the least, not even a dot, looking for one), and therein lay the rumblings of a problem.

Maybe Saul sensed something was up. He frequently broke a silence with, "A penny for your thoughts." God, how I hated that—not so much the clichés he used, but having to censor my reveries. Sometimes I would catch myself in a daydream and wonder, what if Saul asks what I'm thinking? I would then scramble to erase the fantasy and replace it with a selection from my backup list: school, family, weekend plans. Even though I was more likely to be thinking about what to have for lunch than about skinny-dipping with Luke, it put me on edge that at any second Saul might attempt to trespass my mind.

To make matters worse, Saul's sister, Claudia, who had been my high school classmate, confided in us that she had fallen in love with a tall, bearded Gentile professor named Henry at Oberlin where she was a sophomore. "Henry and I sometimes don't realize we've stayed up all night talking till the sun comes up," she told us. In contrast to my safe, Jewish, parent-approved relationship, Claudia's affair percolated with lust and danger.

"I could talk to you all night too," Saul said to me afterwards. Our need to compete romantically with his sister made it all the more obvious that Saul and I were an inferior couple. Not only were we not living together, as Claudia and Henry apparently were, but we also never stayed awake past midnight. Plus, with me cranking out third derivatives until my brain throbbed and him anchored to his quantum applications, we were not accustomed to producing much conversation beyond the occasional groan or huzzah over a failed or successful math computation. Even during meals and car rides, we shared little more than hollow chatter, usually about our plans for the following Saturday night. Sometimes, to relieve the quiet, we made out.

Saul must have had more to say. He was a *Harper's* subscriber, an intellectual compared to me; I never read a book or newspaper unless it was required for class. In high school, I'd never read at all. Maybe it was an undiagnosed learning disability, along with a measure of flexibility on certain matters of conscience, which drove me to cheat my way through subjects like history and biology. For English assignments to read *The Iliad* and *Gulliver's Travels*, I read *Classic Comics* versions instead. Before college, the only lofty scores I came by legitimately were in math and French.

One Saturday Claudia told Saul, "Henry and I are going to elope. When Mom realizes I've disappeared, just tell her I'm okay." Saul tried to talk her out of it, but all she said was, "Henry is my soul mate." The good thing about Claudia's drama was that it gave Saul and me something to talk about. On a Sunday night, a few weeks after spring break, Saul pulled up in front of my dorm to drop me off before heading back to school. As usual, we had spent the weekend alternating between his parents' colonial and my parents' split-level. Gripping the car door handle with one hand, my book bag strap with the other, and looking straight ahead, I said, "I think we need some time apart." He stroked his bottom lip with his ring finger, which gave the unintended impression of an obscene gesture. For a long while he stroked silently. I sat with my teeth clenched, as though waiting for a booster shot.

Finally he said, "I think a trial separation makes sense." *Trial separation!* He made it sound like we were married. Well, regardless of what we called it, I was glad to be granted time off and especially relieved not to have to discuss it. Yet, now that I knew we would be apart, I experienced a stab.

But it was more like a pinprick, because I darted inside and with trembling fingers dialed Luke. Although he and I had not spoken since before I began dating Saul, Luke sounded more amused than surprised to hear from me. I asked when we could get together. "I can't do it this week," he answered. It was impossible that he wasn't aching to see me as much as I was to see him; I was sure he was putting me off just to punish me for all the months I'd spent with Saul. He said we could meet for lunch the following week.

Lunch? I agreed to lunch? Was I in a slumber? And, come to think of it, had I not noticed all the college rah rah going on around me? After all, I had been a social somebody in my high school of hundreds. Now, at Penn, I found myself recast as Saul's steady girlfriend, isolated in a corner of the library with my other new identity as a brain. Admittedly, though, this felt less daunting than trying to catch up on the path toward popularity, and possibly failing, on a campus of thousands.

The day before Luke and I were to have lunch, Saul showed up at my dorm. He assumed that his cutting classes and traveling so far on a weekday would patch things up. It would have been awkward to shatter his enthusiasm by suggesting we prolong the separation. I was more afraid of angering or hurting him than I was of losing him.

Even though it killed me to cancel the date with Luke, it was easier to avoid confrontation and slide back together with Saul than to admit I needed more time. This makeover of me into a slider—doing what was expected of me with an absence of volition—was like I had fallen under a spell the previous September, when the decent, trustworthy, grown-up Saul appeared at the door for our first date.

"Let's open a joint savings account," Saul said, barely able to contain his eagerness. Reflexively, I nodded agreement, trying not to dwell on my back, which felt itchy. That night I dreamed I spotted Luke at the end of a long corridor. Although he was far off, I could see him in microscopic detail: the veins protruding on his large carpenter's hands and the rivets on the pockets of his dungarees erect, like tiny copper nipples. I ran to catch up, my legs spinning fast as pinwheels, but when I got close enough to reach out and grasp his bare, hairless arm, he vanished and I awoke out of breath, clutching the air.

From then on, whenever Saul came to Philly, he picked me up in his Impala and whisked me directly to the drive-in window at PSFS, Philadelphia Saving Fund Society. After depositing leftover allowances, we would marvel at the new total, put the bankbook back in his glove compartment, and then head north to the suburb where our parents lived.

In June the word "engagement" popped up. Marriage was the logical next step, since Saul would be in Philadelphia full time now, attending medical school. "I'll talk to your father,"

Saul said, but to my relief he never got around to it. With the optimism of youth, I put the engagement possibility out of my mind, imagining we could just hum along indefinitely, the way we had been. Maybe Saul felt that way too.

Then, one night in late August, we drove Saul's mother to my parents' house for dinner. As we pulled into the driveway, she opened the glove compartment to look for a pen. Out slid the bankbook onto her lap. Taking one glance at it, she hooted, "Oh! Oh!" and charged up the path, hollering, "Matt, Millie look at this!" Her breathing accelerated as she wagged the small blue book in her outstretched hand.

My parents came running. "Matt," my mother ordered, "take Saul into the den." It was thus that Saul and I became engaged.

The following day Saul's mother ushered him to her jeweler to research diamonds, while my mother marshaled me downtown to Wanamaker's to unearth the perfect black velveteen jumper and ivory satin blouse for the engagement party she had already mapped out in her head. Being engaged felt so enormous and wrong that I couldn't stop shivering, despite ninety-degree weather. I envied every soul I saw for not being in my predicament, even a stringy-haired lady standing beside the department store entrance wearing torn, thick stockings rolled to just below her flabby knees.

It was as if Saul had materialized from a page in my Sociology 101 textbook as my quintessential socio-economic counterpart. I had always wondered who my ideal mate would be, never considering that I would be condemned to a life sentence in Philadelphia with him before I had even declared my major. My parents seemed elated, but I lamented to a friend, "I'm only 18 and already I can see the rest of my days laid out before me."

Why didn't I object? Why would I have agreed to marry someone my parents found so agreeable? Had I been permanently transformed from the devious, fun-loving soul I had been in high school, or was this a temporary aberration?

Major decisions never seemed to be deliberate. If you went with a boy for a year, you got engaged; no one said it was wrong for him to work a trio of fingers into your vagina, but penile penetration had to wait until vows were exchanged in the presence of a rabbi. I went to Penn because if you lived in Philadelphia, you applied to Penn, Temple, and Penn State and if you got into Penn and your father could afford it, you went; I ultimately majored in math, not because I burned to manipulate Fibonacci sequences, but because I had gotten As in high school algebra; and I took teaching courses because my father insisted I have something to fall back on. There was always this falling back, a requirement to stockpile safety nets, as if it were unthinkable to surge through life upright or tilting forward.

One reason I'm sure my folks were so pleased to have this thing tied up was that they were afraid Saul and I would "get into trouble." This was 1964. Co-eds were expected to wear skirts on campus and, contrary to my mother's worst nightmare, I was still a virgin (albeit a "technical virgin").

But how were my parents to know? It was not the kind of thing we discussed at the breakfast table, except for my mother's periodic reports about unwed girls who "got themselves pregnant" then bled to death in dark alleys after going for illegal abortions or sticking wire hangers up their vaginas. As far as I knew, no girl had ever bled to death anywhere but in an alley.

Saul and I had never even discussed having intercourse. It was understood we would wait. Anyway, our passion had peaked in the early months, when the excitement of exchanging touches with someone new masked the flaws that inevitably showed up later. Occasionally Saul tried something a little sexually imaginative, like jiggling my breasts, but it aroused in me only self-consciousness about my body, similar to how I felt in sixth grade when I first began to sprout breasts and would walk hunched over in an attempt to hide them. Finally, I got up the nerve to ask Saul to stop.

At some point UPS cartons containing gifts of chafing dishes and electric knives started piling up in my parents' dining room. Although I had favored a modest celebration, I did not strenuously object to the big affair my mother was orchestrating. It was better than taking the risk I might wake up in the middle of my life regretting I had not had a sit-down roast beef dinner for a considerable segment of Philadelphia's Jewish population.

My mother mailed the hand-calligraphed invitations. And twice a week she drove me to South Philly for a fitting in the living room of the two men she had found to make my cotton-lace, jewel-neck, long-sleeve, A-line, plain, boring gown. I required a custom-made dress, because when we went shopping I was "impossible" and didn't like anything. My aunts threw a kitchen shower, where I stood before eighty women, opening gifts of cooking apparatuses for which I knew neither the names nor the functions. As the stacks of presents grew, I became desensitized to this notion of marriage.

One night after dinner at Saul's parents' house, he called

me into the living room, and before I even sat down he blurted out, "I'm not sure we should get married." I had become so distracted by the prenuptial rumpus that I had ignored how subdued he'd been acting. Now that he acknowledged his reservations, my own foreboding sprang to the surface. We drove in silence for the ten-minute ride to my parents' house. When we reported this new development, they said that perhaps all the tumult was overwhelming, that it was okay if we wanted to have a smaller affair. They suggested we consult a marriage counselor.

Saul and I sat as stiff as cadavers on a worn sofa in Dr. Zisser's cluttered office. "So, what brings you here?" she asked, furrowing her brow and leaning too far forward. With her dark hair wound into a tidy, low bun and the black-rimmed glasses that overpowered her narrow face, she looked like a secretary who stayed late to type a memo for her boss (Cary Grant). When she hands him the completed document, he slides off her spectacles, unclasps her barrette, and the pair fall into a panting embrace.

"Marriage is so final," said Saul, interrupting my matinee. The way he pumped his finger back and forth across his lower lip he must have had more to say, but I prayed he wouldn't; just being in this confession chamber was all the confrontation I could handle. Dr. Zisser turned toward me and raised her eyebrows, apparently my cue.

"I feel bored at times," I said. What I really felt was impaled on one of those fondue forks from the UPS boxes, on the verge of being dunked into a cauldron of bubbling cheese. Dr. Zisser studied us with a grim expression, but provided no answers.

Afterwards Saul and I went for pizza. "What should we

do?" he asked, working a shard of tomato skin from between his top front teeth with his tongue.

Here was my ticket out of the marriage maze, but at that moment all my trapped feelings funneled into one thought: *How would I ever manage to pack up and return all those silver trays?* It would be easier to get divorced and then store the gifts in our parents' basements if things didn't work out.

"I guess we should get married," I replied with the conviction of someone contemplating which head of lettuce to buy.

"What about the big wedding?" he asked. I flashed on what it would be like to recall two hundred and fifty invitations.

"We might as well have it," I said, having just aced a short-answer quiz on Deceiving Myself About the Easy Way Out. Then, in preparation for our wedding night, I placed an Enovid-E, my first birth control pill, onto my tongue and washed it down with a swallow of Coke.

For Saul's bachelor party, his parents organized a barbecue in their backyard. My future father-in-law grilled hamburgers while the guys played Wiffle ball. With bases loaded, the best man swung mightily, accidentally striking Saul with the plastic bat and chipping his front tooth.

When my groom-to-be came over the following morning, I was ecstatic with the rugged look of his new smile, to the extent a boy with dimples could look rugged. At last, a rough edge! You cannot imagine my disappointment when he showed up later with it capped.

On the morning of our wedding day, I returned home from the beauty parlor and brushed out the stiff curls that ringed my face. I then bobby-pinned my hair into a simple knot on top of my head: boring hair to match my boring dress.

My final act before marching to the altar was to sink into my bun the comb attached to my lace-bordered veil and long, billowing train.

Just after my father kissed me, at the very moment he was passing me off to my groom, a ringing sound occurred, along with a wave of chuckles and murmurs throughout the congregation. Saul, with his attraction to gadgets, had not thought to turn off the alarm on his new wristwatch.

Standing beside Saul under the *chuppa*, my life began to pass before me. Suddenly I was ten years old, dribbling a basketball with my twelve-year-old cousin Larry, my idol, in the driveway behind our row houses. As a reward for my improved jump shot, he taught me how to flip a coin so it would always come up heads and how to shift my weight to deliver a wallop when trading punches.

That long strip of pavement was also where I beat up Dickie Rosenstein, stole Harriet Schmerling's valentines, and coaxed Tootsie Weiner to pull down her pants in the back of her parents' garage. I was careful to concentrate on guilt from the distant past, not daring to allow images of Luke, with his chipped-toothed smile and Kennedy jaw, to surface.

After Saul performed the ritual glass smashing with his heel, we embraced for the post-nuptial make-out kiss and turned to walk up the aisle to cries of "*Mazel tov!*" I decided to lighten the mood by stepping up our pace, not realizing my mother—in her cameo as mother of the bride—was fanning out the panel of netting that was to trail behind me. I took my first great stride and my entire headdress popped off, hanging disembodied in my dear mom's hands, a perfect metaphor for my suppressed desire to be unleashed. The crowd's giggles exploded in my ears as two of my bridesmaids gently folded the train and carried it off, like pallbearers transporting a weightless casket.

A few hours into the festivities, while a string of guests were hop-hop-hopping figure eights around the circular dinner tables to the tune of "The Bunny Hop," I slipped away to change into my white linen suit with orange (Saul's favorite color) dots the size of oranges, a white bowler hat, white pumps, and white kid gloves that buttoned with a pearl at the wrist. Saul and I struck a pose for the photographer while zipping my hatbox travel case, and then we made a grand exit, waving good-bye to the guests with arc-shaped motions, like a pair of windshield wipers.

The airport motel was a most unromantic establishment in which to lose my virginity. The brown room, with its dirt-flecked shag rug, artificial wood paneling and mildew-smelling bedspread, seemed more suitable for holing up with an accomplice than with a new husband. While Saul plugged in his electric toothbrush and washed up, I put on the cotton nightgown my mother and I had bought, half-off, at Gimbels. My husband returned from the bathroom, wearing the blue striped shorty pajamas his mother had picked out for him at Brooks Brothers.

"Nice nightgown," he said.

"Nice shorties," I replied.

Then he gave the lamp chain a tug, and we each slipped out of our new night clothes. After folding his PJs and placing them on top of his suitcase, he felt his way onto the bed beside me.

Before I had a moment to worry how this was about to go, he mounted my naked torso and, after a few clumsy attempts, managed to stuff his semi-erect penis into my dry vagina. A slice of light from the parking lot shone through a separation in the curtains, illuminating his ear. To distract myself from the grinding pain, I examined a web of veins in his auricle until abruptly he froze then slumped on top of me, like a deflated blow-up doll.

That's when he admitted he'd had intercourse once before. With an old girlfriend. He had promised her he would never tell. I swore never to tell a soul and then wondered what other secrets he was harboring.

Even though it was three a.m., neither Saul nor I could fall asleep, so we dressed in our twin ensembles—red and white checkered shirts and navy blue Bermudas—and strolled to the airport terminal. It wasn't easy to ignore the raw sensation between my legs. One newsstand was open. Saul bought Playboy; I bought Seventeen.

I had wanted to honeymoon in Banff, but my mother convinced us to go to Miami Beach, saying rates were low in July and that we would be able to afford the newest hotel, The Doral Beach (which a few years later was the setting for the original The Heartbreak Kid, a film about a Jewish guy on his honeymoon who pursues a blonde beauty, played by Cybill Shepherd, while his Jewish bride suffers in bed with severe sunburn). If you were to ask me now, I'd rather stay in a tent in Banff than in the newest hotel in Miami Beach; in fact, I'd rather stay in a tent in Miami Beach.

Each morning upon waking, Saul made me smile when he sang to me in his Bing Crosby tremolo: "Hello Sweetie Peetie. How do you do today? Hello Sweetie Peetie is all I can say." Dinners were harder. The long stretches of silence, with my hands clasped tightly in my lap and nowhere to settle my gaze, made me as uncomfortable as our strained attempts at conversation. What was there to talk about with a person I had spent the entire day next to, doing nothing?

I shouldn't say we did nothing. We played Jotto by the pool. And we took a helicopter ride to get an aerial view of Miami Beach. Although mostly numb to this notion of marriage, I had a faint awareness of pain, as if my whole body had been shot with novocaine that was beginning to wear off. On our final evening, we went to the Playboy Club, where Saul signed up to be a member and bought me a necklace with a delicate silver chain from which hung a diary-sized key embellished with the bunny logo.

The hardest part of being married was knowing ahead of time how each day would turn out. Another challenge was everyone's expectation that I would call my in-laws Mom and Dad. It felt phony to go straight from Mr. and Mrs. to Mom and Dad.

Plus, what I called them had nothing to do with how I felt: I continued to love his father and dislike his humorless, controlling mother. Saul had no trouble using the new monikers for my parents, but I gagged whenever I tried with his parents, so I didn't call them anything, which my mother said was inexcusable.

My concept of marriage was: you do what you want, and I'll do what I want, and if what I want conflicts with what you want, I'm going to do it anyway. That's why, when I finished sewing a red calico valence for the bathroom window at midnight and Saul asked me to wait until morning to hang it, I proceeded to hammer in the curtain rod anyway.

Food became my sole focus. Two years earlier I had sat in class doodling Saul's name in bubble letters; now, at summer school, I filled my notebooks with grocery lists. Unsurprisingly, I gained fifteen pounds. For my non-culinary duties, I came up with shortcuts. When ironing Saul's shirts, for example, I pressed only the collar, cuffs, and triangle part that showed under his blazer.

I also purged our apartment of the paper balls he was fond of making by rolling strips he tore from newspapers between his thumb and forefinger. These little balls were everywhere. If Saul couldn't get his hands on a newspaper, he rotated his fingertips together with nothing between them. Or he caressed his lips, apparently unable to do without the continuous stroking.

The finger revolutions, I suppose, helped provide physical gratification. Every night, as soon as I slipped under the blankets, my eyelids sank with a heaviness I had never known. Slithering up behind me lizard like, Saul would mold himself to me, our bodies forming interlocking Zs.

I would send a message that I wasn't in the mood for sex by not daring to move until after I could feel Saul's muscles relax into slumber. Then I would inch to the precipice on my side of our queen-size bed and ball up with my back to him, my pulse thrumming, as though I had just narrowly escaped Alcatraz. I'd sandwich my head between two pillows and pray for sleep. Seemingly oblivious to the mimed rejection scene the night before, Saul greeted me every morning with the Sweetie Peetie song.

I wondered how anyone managed to remain sexually enthusiastic about the same partner once the newness wore off; it had to be either a big secret or a big lie, like "The Emperor's New Clothes." Sometimes at night, a fierce wind rattled the window glass and whistled through a crack along the sill. With my pillowed head pressed into the lip of my night table, I would shiver in the dark, waiting for the raspy sound of Saul's deep sleep. Then I would reach down to the warm vee between my thighs and press and squeeze until an ecstatic shudder subdued my chill.

One Saturday afternoon, exploding with pent-up appetites, we tore off our clothes and converged on the tangerine-colored, four-seater sofa in the living room for a session of reckless intercourse. For all the intimacy I experienced, I might as well have been humping his electric toothbrush.

Six weeks after swearing till death do us part, Saul and I were in the bedroom of our garden apartment, getting dressed to go to a party for my friend Al, who had just returned from Vietnam. Saul tucked his madras shirt into his khakis and buckled his belt, then sat down on the edge of our bed and quietly told me that he sometimes thought about Babs, a former girlfriend.

Despite all that was amiss about our union, I had folded myself into a wifely mindset. So I was not only surprised but also saddened and wounded in the ego by what I interpreted as his waning interest in me. In my nineteen years, nothing had occurred to demonstrate that his ruminating about another girl meant anything other than a divorce in our future, not that I knew anyone who was divorced. I blew my nose, wiped my tears, and then phoned Al to say something came up and we wouldn't be celebrating with him.

Feeling bad was not part of my repertoire. I barely had to root around for an antidote to Saul's confession: this was my opening to indulge in a full-blown fantasy of my own. It began with driving out of my way to pass Luke's house—the way I had in high school—before returning home from my classes at Penn. When I needed more of a charge, I dialed his number. Then, if he answered, I hung up like a schoolgirl. Oh wait, I was a schoolgirl.

Finally, I confessed the Luke obsession to Saul and we decided I should consult Dr. Zisser, the marriage counselor Saul and I had seen shortly before we wed. Inside her office she studied my figure, which I concealed under a tent-shaped, corduroy jumper. "You need to lose weight, Susan," she said. "And try putting a ribbon in your hair when you wake up." The image of myself twirling around the breakfast table in a frilly bathrobe with a pink bow on my head convinced me to disregard all of her advice.

At the end of the hour she said that if I were to see Luke, to do so in a well-lit restaurant and not to carry out my idea of meeting him in the Philadelphia Museum of Art parking lot. She then admitted that, after Saul and I had visited her, she had not expected us to go through with the marriage. Had it been that obvious? She couldn't have dropped a wee hint?

That evening, when Saul came home, I was setting our small wooden kitchen table with our everyday plates that featured a cheery pattern of tiny strawberries. Saul sat down and asked how my visit with Dr. Zisser went. After I told him— just as we had done a year-and-a-half earlier—we decided to have a trial separation. I would move to my parents' house and work on getting Luke "out of my system."

Once again, Luke did not sound surprised to hear from me, as though he'd been expecting my call. We agreed to meet in the Philadelphia Museum of Art parking lot.

A few nights later, high above the Schuylkill River, where lights from boathouses sparked like shooting stars on the inky water's surface, I lowered myself into Luke's Porsche with my heart galloping. The smell of leather brought back memories of steamy nights with the gearshift jabbing me in the buttocks. I always pulled away before things went too far, so he would respect me for withholding the jewel. He always feigned anger.

"Henceforth misses you," he said. (Did every high school girl have a name for her boyfriend's penis?)

I burrowed my nose into his neck, deeply inhaling its familiar smell of clean sheets. He wrapped both arms around me for a few seconds, then slipped a powerful hand inside the back of my sweater. At the touch of his warm palm against my skin, my body arched with desire so intense it bordered on pain. "I can't believe it's really you," was all I could say. I said it again, as he opened my bra with a flick of his thumb and forefinger.

For a moment I hesitated, savoring my own passion, and then I drew away taking a deep breath. "Listen Luke, I feel too guilty to do anything while I'm still wearing Saul's wedding band," I said as I fumbled to re-fasten the hook.

"So take the ring off," he answered, flashing his chipped-tooth grin. He leaned back in his seat and tapped out a cigarette from a pack of Camels. Was there to be no further sparring? It was not by accident, after all, that I had worn a pullover. What happened to the way he always knew the difference between my no that meant no and my no that meant yes?

I also decided Saul and I shouldn't have sex with each other during the separation. I said it wasn't right if we weren't living together. A product of my fifties upbringing, I believed in this no-sex-unless-living-under-marital-roof rule I had just made up.

Even though Luke was lodged in my thoughts like a splinter you wedge deeper while trying to tweeze it out, Saul's and my trial separation implied we should give the marriage another shot. Plus, Saul's upcoming birthday provided an opportunity to get the dog I had been wanting ever since my mother gave away our black mutt, Pepper, whom she replaced with a new pair of ice skates that I never grew into.

So rather than slipping out of the marital noose, I bought an eight-week-old collie mix, tied a wide orange bow around my neck, another around the puppy's with a card that said "Happy Birthday! Love, Sweetie Peetie and Boswell," and moved back in.

A few weeks later I wanted to get a Christmas tree. All my life my mother had told me, "When you get married, you can have a tree." Now I was married and my husband refused to allow it on the same grounds that we were Jewish. To satisfy my attraction to tinsel, I scattered strips of foil around the base of our clothes tree and hung red and green Christmas balls from the curtain rods, the kitchen cabinet knobs, and from my earlobes.

On top of everything else, my girlfriend told me about a new dating service that used computers to match people up. I was dying to try it. I realize this may sound wacky, but I was not expecting to date anyone, only to see who my ideal mate was. Computers were relatively new and totally mysterious, almost holy, in their capacity to perform miracles. I believed they could track down my soul mate the same way, when I was eleven, I had believed that praying to God could make Herb Score, the Cleveland Indians pitcher, not go blind after he got hit in the face with a line drive.

Saul brushed it off as ridiculous when I proposed the dating service idea. But I started daydreaming about it until I could no longer stand not knowing what the computer would tell me. After all, you spend your entire life knowing your destiny is out there, pulling on his socks every morning. Along comes the opportunity to find this guy. It kept playing in my head, like in the song, "They never met, they never kissed. And they will never know what happiness they missed. For she lived on the morning side of the mountain and he lived on the twilight side of the hill." I had to find out who he was.

I decided to fill out the Operation Match application, figuring I would be able to retrieve the list of names from the mail without Saul knowing. In order to see whether we would be assigned to each other, I filled out an application for Saul too, stating his preferences for folk tunes, naïve art, and the color orange.

The call came in the evening. Saul was hunched over the kitchen table scooping vanilla fudge ice cream from the carton into his mouth with a soup spoon; I was curled up on the sofa, reading noodle pudding recipes from a cookbook compiled by the sisterhood at my parents' synagogue. I shuffled into the bedroom to answer the phone.

"Hello, is Sue there?" a deep voice asked.

"This is Sue."

"Hi, I'm Ron," the voice said. "You're on my list from Operation Match."

Why hadn't it occurred to me that boys would be calling our apartment? I had to get rid of him, but I also had to know more.

"Listen, Ron, I can't talk now. Can I call you tomorrow? Wait a minute. What's your number? I haven't gotten my printout yet."

He recited his phone number and then added, "I'll be away until a week from Sunday. I'm going skiing in Aspen."

That did it. The only time I ever skied was when I was fifteen, during a weekend at The Concord in the Catskills with my parents. I longed to ski again, but because Saul's life rarely extended beyond the covers of *Gray's Anatomy*, the sportiest activity we ever undertook was going to the trotters, once, where I nagged him to stop betting so much.

"Who was that?" Saul asked, walking in just as I hung up. He puckered his lips to one side then the other to wipe fudge from the corners of his mouth with his fingertip.

I confessed about applying to the dating service, hoping he would be the one to say we should call it quits. Sounding apologetic rather than hurt or angry, he stated the obvious, "I guess it's just not working out between us."

We gave Boswell to my cousin and stored all the china, CorningWare, and silver trays in my parents' basement, because my mother said Saul would get married again and have another big wedding with gifts. (I know, that makes no sense.) Forty years later, having schlepped the silver trays during countless moves from one residence to another, without ever removing them from the initial brown packing paper, I gave them to a crew of moving men.

Six months after marrying Saul, it was as though I had been released from inside a jar, like a lightning bug. Now, everything the world had to offer seemed possible: I was Susan Fishman again! From the hall in my dorm, I phoned Ron. On our date, I noticed he had this annoying way of licking his Tastykake wrapper.

DIZZY
1967 - 1968

I emerged from the husband, the garden apartment, the Impala sedan, and the color orange squinting at the sudden brightness of university life. Rubbing my palms in anticipation of the fun in store, I climbed back into the skin I had shed when I first met Saul, nearly two and a half years earlier, and landed with a bounce in an apartment dorm. At age twenty, for the first time ever, I was untethered—even my parents were not near enough to control my moves. Which is not to say they didn't try. They warned me not to date for a couple of months; it wouldn't look right, they said, because divorce proceedings had only just begun. Yet I saw no reason to stifle my social life. After all, I was not in mourning. Quite the contrary. The only restriction it seemed I would have to endure was curfew. It did not take long to figure out, however, that if I did not sign out of my dorm when I went on a date, I would not have to sign back in.

While married, I had imagined the wild campus social scene I was missing. Now I found that fraternity parties—where beer-sodden big shots and their ample-breasted dates shimmied in dark, airless rooms—offended every one of my senses, even though I wished I could fit in. Knowing this fun was going on without me felt like I had lost my way to a dance marathon that I desperately wanted to get to, but did not want to be at. Maybe I could acquire a taste for noise and sweat.

I feared I might disappear altogether in Penn's hugeness. During the time I had commuted between school and the calico-curtained apartment I shared with Saul, college had been nothing more than the library, a few ivy-draped walls, and a pharmacy known as The Dirty Drug, where I could buy a hamburger for thirty-five cents. It was startling to become available and discover I was no longer sought after the way I had been in high school, no longer able to take popularity for granted. The Wharton boys apparently had not been waiting for Susan Fishman to wangle out of her marriage; most now appeared to have girlfriends, stiffly-coiffed coeds who pranced across campus flaunting fraternity pins on their cashmere breasts, engaged to be engaged. Some girls wore multi-carat, pear-shaped diamonds on their left hands. I wondered whether any of them had a clue as to what they were in for.

I met Dizzy in the fall of 1966, my senior year of college, nine months after my starter marriage ended. Most evenings I found him at the pinball machine in the deli across from my apartment. If I dallied beside him, looking on, every so often he would reward me with a turn at the flippers.

One night, at around eleven, he asked if I wanted to join him and his roommates for their nightly card game. After several days he stopped asking; he assumed I would tail behind him to join the guys, which included getting high on marijuana and gorging on the standard fare of Oreos, hoagies dripping with mayo, and pints of vanilla fudge we passed around like joints to scoop directly into our mouths. Most of the boys had nicknames that were shortened versions of their last names: Bo, Rose, Duck. Me they called Fish.

Whenever Dizzy saw me on campus, he greeted me with a jab to the triceps and a "Hey, Fish." On a bench outside the library, I confessed to Bo my acute attraction to Dizzy, his slender body and smooth, long arms with not too many muscles and his reddish-brown hair—unruly like him—that matched his eyes. Even his thick Brooklyn accent enchanted me. Bo and I hatched a scheme that entailed my "coincidentally" being in New York on a weekend when Diz was going home.

"I'm going to the city on Saturday," I said nonchalantly the following Tuesday.

"Me too," Dizzy said. "Why don't we get together?" It worked!

For the remainder of the week, thoughts of our date consumed me: what I would wear, what I would talk about, and how it would feel to kiss Dizzy's impish, freckled face. If my sister had dropped dead that Friday, I cannot say for certain whether or not it would have tempered my delirium.

On Saturday at my girlfriend's mother's Upper East Side apartment, I applied perfumes, powders, and sprays and then slipped into a skimpy burgundy velour shift with cap sleeves, which I had sewn from a Simplicity pattern, and brand new matching Pappagallo one-inch heels with grosgrain bows at the toe.

I waited for Dizzy beside the door of the Howard Johnson's at Times Square, nervously yanking up my garter belt. He arrived fifteen minutes late.

"Hey, Fish. You look nice," he said, sounding surprised. "Let's grab a burger here before the movie." He did not deliver the usual blow to my upper arm, which suggested the evening had promise.

Three hours later, parked opposite a warehouse near Tenth Avenue, we were panting heavily in the back seat of his father's winged pink Cadillac. On the ride back to my friend's, it was awkward to straddle the border between buddy and girlfriend; how was I to act, having gone from one role to the other during a single evening? "Hey Fish, how come you're so quiet?" Dizzy asked, which made me even more uncomfortable.

"I don't know," I mumbled with uncharacteristic shyness.

I felt a similar unease at the card game the following Monday with Dizzy's arm slung over my shoulder, everyone looking at me, as if I had paraded in with my eyebrows shaved off. The previous week I was like a fraternity brother; now suddenly, I was a girl. By the following day, though, everyone had become used to my being Dizzy's sidekick. What I could not get used to was Diz calling me Fish in bed.

We were in bed a lot. Some nights Dizzy would leap off the mattress we shared in his laundry-strewn room, furious with me for not going all the way. Being abandoned like that, my naked body twisted in those stinking, crumpled sheets, filled me with self-pity. A good time abruptly gone sour gave the worst kind of letdown.

Having experienced only marital sex, I had reverted to a chaste mentality. I remained unyielding in Dizzy's bed for weeks. One night, for no particular reason, I did not resist. For the next twenty-four hours, wherever we went, I clung to him as though he were still inside me.

Shortly thereafter, Dizzy admitted I was the first girl he

had ever slept with. He also started teasing me about being "used goods," which made it obvious how much it bothered him that I'd had more sex than he'd had. It didn't bother me. He scored higher at pinball; I had gotten laid more times.

I didn't know any other couples at school who were living together in 1967. Cohabiting was not something I had decided to do: rather, it just happened. I never wanted to go back to my place, so I didn't. This caused one enormous problem for me: fear of my father's rage. A few years later living with a boy was not a big deal, but in 1967, for the daughter of Matt Fishman, it was a crime of scary magnitude.

There were no such things as answering machines, so I would guess when my parents might call, and I'd sit all evening in my room to keep up the charade that I lived there. Most of my waking hours, I felt like puking up the guilt and lies.

Whenever I was about to visit my parents, I had to get a Valium from my girlfriend to turn off the garbage disposal that was grinding away at my vital organs. Sometimes I wished my mother and father would die. I formed a mental image of an instantaneous, painless death. A car crash. That way they would never get wind of my wayward behavior, and I would be spared their wrath and disappointment.

Finally, I could no longer bear the dread that they might find out about Dizzy. So one Sunday afternoon Dizzy and I traveled to the suburbs to confess.

Mom, Dad, Dizzy, and I each sat with our hands in our laps on the nubby violet sectional couches in the den. "What part of Brooklyn are you from?" my mother asked Dizzy, interrupting the silence.

"Do you know Brooklyn?" he asked.

"No," she answered.

With an insulting chuckle, he started naming the streets that intersected Flatbush Avenue in the neighborhood where he grew up.

That's when I spit out, "We're living together."

My father remained mute. For the first time in my life, I prayed he would fly into a tirade, one with enough power to shatter the brick I felt in my chest. My mother recited an uncharacteristically emotional speech, saying she would give her life for me to be happy. Why couldn't she be the silent one? I sat stiffly, digging the raw stumps that had once been my fingernails into my thighs. I prayed no one would cry.

There was nothing else to say. My parents had always told me, "No matter what, you'll always be our daughter." They made good on that. No threats or severances. Maybe, in a way, they were relieved. For months they surely knew from my limited communication that something was up; God knows what they had imagined. At least Dizzy was Jewish. Their sadness was my punishment.

After graduation, Dizzy and I set up housekeeping in a garden apartment in Northern Virginia, not unlike the one I had lived in with Saul, and a ten-minute commute to George Washington University where Dizzy attended law school. I took a job as a math instructor at the local community college. Some evenings Diz and I invited Bo, who lived downstairs, for my specialty, Aztec meat pie: a pungent mixture of ground chuck, onion flakes, ketchup, and cheddar cheese baked in a round cake tin. The highlight of each day was watching Perry Mason reruns before bed.

One Sunday in October my parents visited. Although they arrived in time for lunch and stayed until dark, the main thing I remember about that afternoon is the way they padded past our bedroom, peeking in as though it were roped off like a museum display. From behind them, I watched in horror as the double bed seemed to inflate, practically oozing into the hallway.

The whole thing felt reminiscent of my marriage—the apartment, the meat pie, and the monotonous sex. Living at college with Dizzy and his roommates had been so much more fun. Had there been an exact moment that the Q-tips Dizzy left on the bathroom sink, yellow with earwax, began to make me cringe? Why had I been able to ignore them before?

There was also the Robert Zweben problem. Had it been before the luster with Dizzy started to fade that I first spotted Robert in the law library? Or had I already become disenchanted with Dizzy and, thus, vulnerable to the swagger of someone else's narrow hips?

It did not help that Dizzy had a practice of squeezing the inside of my thigh, which I hated so much that I would jump if he just touched my leg. When I begged him to abandon the pinching, he ignored me. It reminded me of Mr. Mazza, my piano teacher when I was thirteen, who used to stroke that same patch of skin to the boogie-woogie beat of the music I played.

After a while, I did not want Dizzy to touch me at all. When I told him I wanted out from the relationship, he promised to discontinue the thigh squeezing if I would stay. But it was too late.

Shortly after I moved into a Georgetown townhouse with three other girls, Dizzy joined a commune where he smoked dope and ate macrobiotic foods. His new girlfriend, a dark, Greek beauty named Fern, walked barefoot and wore filmy, white toga-like garments. Later, I heard Diz was living on a mountaintop in California where he worked as a financial advisor to the Maharaj Ji.

I've always been grateful for my starter marriage; otherwise, Dizzy might have become my starter husband.

SHELLS
1968–1977

Once again I was unshackled—flying solo—extricated from parents, school, and romantic entanglements. These carefree single years began around the time women's lib was taking hold and before anyone ever heard of AIDS, a slice of time that fostered sexual freedom without life-threatening consequences.

I spent a lot of time in cafes and pubs with one or another of a dozen intimates, both male and female, talking about boys over onion soup, quiche, and Chablis. The subject never wore thin. That's how I stumbled upon Billy Kiefer, a waiter whose thick, straight, blonde hair fell across his forehead and grazed his Aryan cheekbones each time he placed a draft on someone's table. I liked having a crush as accessible as Billy.

While Glen Campbell crooned "Where's the Playground, Susie?" on the jukebox, I would follow Billy with my eyes—brooding and sipping wine in a corner booth with a friend, running through scenarios of how Billy and I would eventually get together. Even though the only words Billy and I ever exchanged related to drink orders, I was so lovesick that I lost eight pounds and wrote his name with eyeliner in each of the three bathroom stalls.

After weeks of this ogling, I learned from one of his co-workers that Billy's house was only a block from mine, more than a coincidence to someone like me who kept a copy of Linda Goodman's *Sun Signs* on the night table. The following Saturday, I set my alarm for eight a.m. After washing my hair, curling it with hot rollers, and slipping into my favorite jeans, I walked to the convenience store that was midway between our houses, certain Billy would drop in for coffee or the paper. Everyone did. After I had consumed three cups of coffee, he finally appeared. Instantly I stopped noticing how badly I had to pee and instead began to quake; all the caffeine coupled with the sight of him overtook my anatomy.

I rose from my post on a tomato sauce carton and gingerly stepped over the pile of newspapers I had been reading. Trying to seem nonchalant, I said, "Hi," and then froze with the thought that I might not be able to get anything else to come out.

"Hi," he replied in a way that sounded more like a question than a greeting. "What are you doing here?"

"I live around the corner," I managed, relieved that at least he recognized me.

"Me too." He seemed genuinely pleased. "Listen, I get off early tomorrow. Do you want to meet me at work? Around six? We can go to dinner."

"Sure," I said, dying. "My name's Susan, by the way."

"I know. I'm Billy."

"Hi. I mean bye," I answered, and then ran out the door.

A few minutes later, standing before my bathroom mirror, I winked at my reflection and let out a whoop. Then I phoned my girlfriend, who was studying for her master's degree in psychology. She told me I had a Casanova Complex.

Over dinner that Sunday, I confessed to Billy how I had swooned from afar while he waited tables and how I had plotted the Saturday morning stakeout. Part of the thrill of a first date with a conquest was weaving this pre-date history into the conversation. On our second date I showed him the hearts I had drawn above the toilet paper rolls in the ladies room, all the while oozing this unspoken Isn't it amazing, and now here we are together? I waited to hear the fantasies he'd had about me, but they never came.

Billy and I had so few mutual interests that I kept a list of topics to talk about by the phone for when he called. Billy was still in college and stood almost as tall as my five feet five; it was satisfying to embrace someone my own size, like matching pieces of a jigsaw puzzle. Our dates usually began before Billy's shift was over. We would have dinner in the restaurant's kitchen, standing while eating leftovers from his customers' plates. Funny that I thought nothing of polishing off a half-eaten lamb chop, given my reluctance forty years later to dip a carrot stick into a bowl of hummus for fear someone had double-dipped. After these second-hand kitchen dinners, we would double date with Billy's roommate and, since I was the only one with a car, everyone would squeeze into my VW. I felt like their chaperone.

Boys like Billy, who had nothing that interested me other than pleasing appearances, I called shells. Relationships with shells had contrived beginnings and no particular endings. What mattered was demonstrating to myself that I could arouse the boy's interest. If we stopped seeing each other, I could always capture another shell—they were everywhere. (I suspected they felt the same about me.) I would spot a boy with possibilities, then target him to be the center of a whole fiction. It was like some horror film where the demon selects its prey, traps it, and then finally destroys it. But, in fact, what I loved about these boys was that they had no feelings; there was never any pain on either side; neither they nor I cared much about what happened between us beyond the following Saturday night.

On the other hand, breaking up with someone who was more than a shell was an ordeal, especially if I were the one saying good-bye. It was so difficult for me to tell a boy I had lost interest that I was likely to avoid him altogether by purposely staying out late every night and not answering my phone when I was home. I doubt that I can take credit for an altruistic aversion to inflicting pain. It is more likely I was afraid of confrontation, of getting bawled out.

When a boy I liked ditched me, I wallowed in the bitter-sweet flavor of my tears, as though I were the spurned sweet-heart in a love comic. I would feel sorry for my sad reflection in front of the very same mirror I winked at every time I landed a decent date. Then, after being weepy for a few days, I'd be out somewhere and spot a replacement. Though I believed I would never tire of this succession of shells, after I met Jeff, all that changed. But I'm getting ahead of myself.

SHRINKS ARE LIKE BOYFRIENDS WHO CAN'T DUMP YOU
1967–1976

I went through psychiatrists the same way I went through boys. Therapy had been my parents' way of disciplining me: you act up, you go back to Dr. Stephenson. When I was living with Dizzy, I thought it would smooth things over with my parents if I went to a therapist. I used the doctors to soften the blow to them, an insanity plea that I could not be held responsible for my actions. My father never objected to paying the bills.

Dr. Amsterdam resembled Art Buchwald, but without the cigar. In his office, pastel-colored prints in cheap frames hung on the walls. A peach leather couch and a glass coffee table with chrome legs shared terrain on a large, faux Oriental rug. I was glad Amsterdam had me lie on the couch; that way I did not have to look at him while peeling myself apart like an onion (his metaphor, not mine).

Confessing details of my sex life to a stocky Jewish man my father's age, seemed perverted.

As a topic, I preferred death. I shared with Dr. A some of my elaborately spun fantasies about my untimely end, especially the funeral. With the little I had learned in Psych I, plus what I picked up from lying like a corpse on Amsterdam's couch, I postulated that either my guilt was so acute that I was trying to kill myself by drifting to these burial scenes, or that my rage—of which I was unaware—was so profound that I delighted in cranking out these reruns of my parents' sorrow.

"Whenever you catch yourself in a morbid fantasy," he said, "cut it right off. Changing takes time, but you'll get the hang of it. It's like trying to adjust to a new way of gripping a golf club. You shift your hands and at first it feels awkward."

At this point he stood up and stepped into my line of vision to demonstrate, his fleshy, white, manicured fingers squeezing an imaginary golf club. "After a while it becomes second nature," he said, flicking his wrists to tap his pretend ball into an invisible hole on the Oriental before he faded behind my head again.

His shtick was starting to bore me. "I've decided to take a break from therapy," I told him the following week.

"This doesn't surprise me, Susan. It's the easy way out to run away from your problems." I later learned that's what they all said when you quit.

I had no intention of giving up therapy; I wanted only to give up Amsterdam. After Dizzy and I broke up I continued seeing shrinks. Friends drank or smoked dope to get high, while I became intoxicated by going to therapy.

My quest to bounce through life with no limits on fun inspired my mother to insert into every phone conversation the question, "Why do you have to be such an extremist, Susan?" as if I were an assassin with straps of bullets crisscrossing my chest. Was I afraid that without the euphoria and without the shrinks, I would be sucked into a sinkhole?

Dr. Miller was as different from Amsterdam as Sigmund Freud was from Ann Landers. I first met Michael Miller at the psychodrama he conducted every Tuesday night in his office. His small dark eyes formed a permanent squint on his round face, which made him appear to be in perpetual thought. With those eyes, his pointed nose, and pursed mouth, he looked rather like an intelligent weasel. Wisps of white hair stood up on his bald head.

On my first visit to the psychodrama, I volunteered to play the role of mother for one of the regulars. During excessive applause for our performance, I turned to Dr. Miller, "I'd like to do a scene with my father."

"Okay. You play your father," he said. "Who wants to play Susan?" A tiny, olive-skinned girl with hollow eyes raised her hand. "Come on up here, Cathy," crooned Miller, his quiz-show-host manner canceling out his cerebral appearance.

Cathy and I sat facing each other, surrounded by a U of onlookers.

"Susan," I began. "I hope you're not going to move in with another boy."

"Why Dad?" Confronted with this open-ended question, I could tell Cathy had experience in psychodramatics.

"You'll get yourself into trouble. Plus, how does it look for my daughter to be living with a boy?"

The exchange lacked the gusto of my real-life exchanges with Dad, which convinced me that in the future I would attend these exhibitions as a voyeur rather than as a participant. Before leaving, I made an appointment to see Miller privately.

Dr. Miller seemed pleased that I wanted to become his private patient. When I walked into his office for my initial

SUSAN ORLINS

consultation, he hugged me—too long and too hard. As I
unfolded the story of my life, he kept interrupting to tell me
about his amorous triumphs.

"Sex can be so beautiful, Susan. You know, I have given
women orgasms that have lasted twenty minutes." Was I supposed to feel inadequate? Or that I was missing out on something? I nodded politely, thinking he's full of baloney. Because
he was so weird, I made an appointment to see him again.
And again. Before each session, he gave me the awful hug and
then another at the end of the hour. I would have felt rude to
say no to the doctor's hugs and orgasm updates.

It was a matter of pride for me to make my visits engag-
ing, though I was not always successful. One afternoon I an-
nounced I had a crush on a colleague at the community college where I taught math; he was a sociology professor named
Bob with skin so soft and white it seemed you would leave a
dent if you pressed it with your thumb. "Maybe I can get my
friend Ann to invite him to her brunch this Sunday," I said.

Miller's eyes floated upward and disappeared under his veiny
lids, and then his chin fell to his chest. I tried to fill the silence.
"Um, wouldn't that be a good way to get Bob to notice me?"

After a pause, pretending Miller hadn't fallen asleep, I answered myself, "I think I should do it."

"Dr. Miller?"

"Put the plane in the hangar," he mumbled.

"What?" I said, even though I knew he was dreaming out
loud. My sexless ramblings had bored him into narcolepsy.
What was the protocol? To stay? Would he charge me?

Finally I shouted, "I have to leave." With a gurgling sound,
he pulled himself up and lumbered over to hug me good-bye.

I don't know what kept me going back every week for

months. Was it the same inertia that glued me to relationships long after the melody had petered out? Breaking up with a therapist, unlike breaking up with a boy, had the advantage that, if I wanted, I could do it without confrontation by leaving a message with the answering service.

The telephone breakup tempted me every time. You knew shrinks were able to tolerate rejection or at least act as though they were; you could count on them to analyze the severance but not to chastise. So I often allowed a whole session to announce and discuss a termination, giving the therapist ample opportunity to convince me not to dump him. They all tried, while I leaned back in my chair nodding. But none succeeded, ultimately proving they were right about my need to control. I could stroll off, whistling that I had given the guy a fair shake, even paid him for it, and I could feel secure he would never call the way a boy might once it was over.

With Miller I hung on because I persuaded myself that his unconventional approach might trigger a spark in my outer limits, territory that was closed to ordinary psychiatrists as well as to me so far. Although I declined his suggestion to join his nude group sessions, I agreed to hypnosis. I couldn't help wondering whether he might put me under and then try one of his interminable orgasms on me, so I always kept an eye slit open.

Dr. Miller treated me during what I called my re-virgination phase. His theme that I should relinquish this hold on what I considered my virginity—given that I'd only ever had marital or living together sex—tempted me. "Just find a boy, any boy, and go to bed with him," he pleaded.

Maybe the repeated tales of his torrid sexual encounters were beginning to whet my appetite—not for him, yuck, but for someone. Or perhaps because it was the seventies and everyone appeared to be doing it, I was becoming deprogrammed from a lifetime of my mother's sex-avoidance coaching.

One morning over my daily soft-boiled egg and toast I read a profile in The *Washington Post* about Dr. Butler, a psychiatrist whose patient list, it said, included ambassadors, senators, news anchors, and even movie stars. Immediately I phoned for an appointment. Maybe I would see someone famous in the waiting room. Plus, I always got good hairdressers from newspaper articles.

Butler greeted me in his office with a handshake, and then cut an arc in the air with his upturned palm to offer me my choice of seats. It was impossible not to notice his perfect posture and overly starched shirt, as if his stiff clothing were holding him upright. I settled into a high-backed recliner, pulled up a leather ottoman for my feet, and began to recite my boyfriend history.

I could never quite ignore the Kleenex boxes that sat on mahogany coffee tables within arm's reach of every seat in every doctor's office. They stood like intruders, eavesdroppers, jurors at the ready, challenging me to wonder whether I was devoid of emotion. Did the fact that I never had tears to dab mean I was a failure at therapy?

Sometimes I felt foolish clucking on about my merry life. And sometimes I thought that if just once I could cry, it would do away with my desire (need?) ever to see another shrink.

Butler sat like a tree trunk, studying me through thick black-rimmed glasses, never uttering a word. I was uncomfortable without feedback—I wanted to jar him into saying what he thought. Usually I could detect signs the therapist was at least entertained. When I finished my tale, near the end of the second visit, he finally spoke. "You've told me about this boy, that boy, and the other boy, but what about Susan Fishman? What about Susan Fishman?"

It was the first time anyone had confronted me with the notion of defining myself separately from the boys I had dated. I had not a glimmer as to what the answer was supposed to be, but I lacked the patience to have the mute Dr. Butler help me find out.

Before he fled the country as a result of tax evasion charges, my girlfriend's shrink supplied her with the name of a female psychiatrist in Northern Virginia. Even though the referral came from a fugitive psychiatrist who slept with his patients, I was curious to give a woman doctor a try. Doris Woodward was about fifty years old, my mother's age, and looked so much like Doris Day that I kept imagining her in a bubble bath, sweet-talking Rock Hudson on a pink Princess phone.

"I come twice a week and I like a doctor who speaks," I told her at the end of the first session.

Her face brightened with that *Pillow Talk* smile. "I speak plenty, but you don't need to come twice a week. I'll see you next Wednesday at the same time."

This surprised me—one, because all the others had me coming twice a week and two, because she apparently was not going to let me be the decider. Why had my previous shrinks required me to see them so often? Did they need the business? No doubt they would say that I now required only weekly visits due to the success of their therapies.

The more I got to know Dr. Woodward, the more we bonded. I had no frame of reference for our kind of attachment, which felt like a mother-daughter relationship, but one that allowed me to confide in her and not be judged. Perhaps she mothered me too much, counseling rather than allowing me to dig for my own conclusions. Often, having listened to one of my reports, she would start with, "Now see here, Susan, why don't you . . . ." I always left her office in particularly high spirits, the way you feel after spending the day with a friend who appreciates you and brings out your best. After several months, I began to worry what would happen if I ever finished my therapy. I made believe we would always be friends, in a parent and child way but without the angst.

Because she had no children, I speculated that I had already become a surrogate daughter for her. I thought about her having no kids all the time. Despite the feminist movement, I could not fathom that anyone would be childless by choice. However, I was afraid to ask about it, believing she must have had a child who had died and I could not bear to see sorrow on her pretty, freckled face.

The privacy barrier that a patient was not supposed to overstep felt as if psychiatrists and I were on opposite sides of a one-way mirror—okay for them to know every humiliating yen I'd ever entertained, but I was to expect no information about their lives. Dr. Woodward was different. She allowed me a peek into her personal world, her favorite topics being her horses and Dobermans as well as the rugged canoe and scuba diving trips she took with her husband. Unafraid of admitting that she too was prone to excess, she acknowledged that she consumed twelve cans of Pepsi (never Coke) every day.

"Even when Jim and I trek to the far reaches of Canada, we always tote my cases of Pepsi," she said after one of her vacations. Her eyes shone with a conspiratorial twinkle, as if to say, *See? I'm a little nuts, just like you.*

After I had been going to her for a year or so she told me that Martha, one of her Dobermans, was sick. "Jim and I won't be able to travel anymore. Martha needs to be spoon-fed and won't accept food from anyone but me." Every night I prayed that Martha wouldn't die. Subsequently, Dr. Woodward limited her personal talk to the subject of animals—facts, never feelings—narrated with Doris Day charm.

It was 1975, the spring I met Chevalier Gabay at the public tennis courts around the corner from the narrow Georgetown house I shared with two other girls. Chev was an easy-going, wiry Jamaican with high cheekbones and missing teeth that gave him the appearance of a jack-o-lantern. Not at all self-conscious about the spaces in his gums, his mouth was typically open with laughter.

Sometimes Chev looked after me the way a parent would. When I was in bed with the flu, he concocted a tea from herbs and Grand Marnier that cleared my head; on my VW's temperamental days, Chev could cure whatever ailed the eleven-year-old car just by tinkering; and he took a mother's pleasure in getting me to eat tuna fish, mashing it with chopped tomatoes and warm hard-boiled eggs.

Other times, I took care of him. Chev was homeless—by choice. With a free-spirit of the seventies, he delighted in being unencumbered by living quarters and possessions. If he did not have a current mate, he would appear on the doorstep of his former girlfriend, Cindi, and she always took him in. When he needed cash, he drove a taxi; otherwise he hung out at friends' apartments, sometimes not showing up at my place for days.

I'd never had a boyfriend this aloof. I puzzled about how

to deal with him, as well as how to contain my jealousy, since I suspected he was passing time in Cindi's bed. With Chev, I never got the chance to have the upper hand; he controlled the flow of our relationship. During his absences, I could not stop obsessing about whom he was with.

I came up with a plan for Dr. Woodward to cure my heartache. "I want to be like the Jamaican women Chev tells me about, who turn their heads the other way when their boyfriends or husbands screw around," I told her. My idea was that a psychiatrist ought to be able to mold my mind, the way a plastic surgeon could change a person's nose.

"Now see here, Susan," she said, "you are not a Jamaican woman. You have a right to expect fidelity from your man. Let's find out just who Susan Fishman is and learn to accept that." It sounded like an echo of Dr. Butler's words, but this time I was willing to comply. Shifting into cheerleader mode, she continued, "Come on, now. You don't have to put up with this. You have so much going for you: you're smart, you're attractive, you're sensitive, and athletic, and resourceful." During every session she worked a list like this into the conversation.

The fear of my parents discovering I was dating a black guy was so intense, I wasted little time in revealing it to them. Also, I figured I had to hurry in case someone who knew my parents were to stumble upon Chev and me sharing a platter of rice and black beans at our favorite Cuban restaurant; I felt certain such news would carry swiftly to the suburbs of Philadelphia.

Yet how could I possibly confess to my parents, knowing what their reaction would be? I did not want to see their eyes when they found out. Or be a captive audience for their rebuke. I took the cowardly path of enlisting my brother to confess for me.

While I paced in my living room a hundred and fifty miles away, he drove to our parents' house on a Saturday night and waited for them to come home from a party. To calm myself, I resorted to the same positive spin as I had with the Dizzy confession, that they would be relieved to know why I'd been so detached lately. The last time they had driven home to find Mark waiting in the house was when my Uncle Irv had died; they had been in Washington that day visiting me. So this time when my father pulled his Cadillac into the driveway, and they saw Mark's car, they braced themselves.

After telling our parents about Chev, my brother called me from a pay phone, the way a hit man might, to say he had finished the job, "How did they take it?" I asked.

Mark's report was chilling: "Daddy immediately said, 'I knew it.' He told me that when he was shaving this morning, he looked in the mirror and said to himself, 'He's black. Susan has a boyfriend and he's black.' Mommy said it could have been worse. She thought I was there to tell them someone had died."

After we hung up, I was still trying to digest Mark's words when the phone rang again. It was my father. He got right to the point.

"Did you have sex with him?"

"Yes."

"When did you start having sex with him?"

"On the first date," I answered, barely audibly, surprising myself by having answered at all. It had not actually been a date. Chev and I had been playing tennis together nearly every day for months; on many warm evenings we hung out at the courts for hours. One afternoon we played a match and then walked to my house for some water. Soon we were in my bed, his narrow, bony brown hips pressed into my soft white belly.

What masochistic weakness made my father ask? Maybe it was his optimism that allowed him to believe my reply would be the one he wanted to hear or that Mark's report had been grossly overstated.

And what sadistic streak in me allowed such a response? Why was I incapable of lying about this? I could color any other story to deceive my parents, but my guilty romances seemed to form their own separate category for truth-telling.

"Susan," he said, sounding graver than I had ever heard him. "You're going to have to choose: him or us. We want what's best for you, and seeing this boy can only hurt you. You think about it and I'll call you tomorrow."

There was nothing to think about. Anyway, Dad had to have been bluffing. Jewish parents did not disown their kids—they didn't even send them away to boarding school. Even if I had wanted to come around to my father's way of thinking, which was impossible, I would never have permitted him to dictate how I ran my life. Nonetheless, I was haunted by what he had said, "seeing this boy can only hurt you," not only the words he had spoken but also the dark tone his voice had shifted into when he said it.

What kind of hurt was he talking about? Was he so offended I was dating a black guy that he was willing to give up his own daughter? I had never thought of my father as prejudiced. What ever happened to: *You can always come to us, no matter what?*

On weekdays, when my father was at his office, I sneaked phone calls to my mother. It did not occur to me until years later that she was probably reporting back to my father how I was doing. Her take on the whole thing was different from his. She may have been pretending disdain for my father's sake, but I could tell that her objections were not from the heart. Once she said, "I understand how you would find a black man attractive. Like Harry Belafonte." I soon realized my dad had not been bluffing, and being fatherless became a way of life with a big hole in it.

My frustration with my father's narrow-mindedness trumped my sadness at the loss of him, until the night I went to see the movie, *Fiddler on the Roof*. Toward the end, Tevye said, "My daughter is dead," referring to Chava, who had married a Gentile boy. Chava knelt, weeping in an open field after her father had pushed his cart past her as though he were sightless and she were no more than so many dewdrops in the gray mist. My tears paralleled hers. The credits ran, the lights came on, but I could not stop sobbing. Tevye's words, "If I try and bend that far I'll break," played over and over in my mind. It was the first time I had stopped thinking about myself and my values long enough to imagine how distraught my father must have felt.

Since I no longer visited Philadelphia, I did not see my sister or brother. My brother told me that whenever the family got together, my name never came up. If I had died, I believed my father would have kept my memory alive. I prayed no one would really die before we had a chance to reconcile.

While interracial couples were becoming less rare in 1970s Washington, Chev and I attracted stares wherever we went. I enjoyed that kind of attention but tried to appear cool and nonchalant. Even if I did not catch people looking at us, I knew they were, because I can tell you how it feels to have a hundred eyes dancing on your back.

One place where nobody's head ever turned to notice Chev and me was at Tasso's, a basement bar, where we often hung out on wobbly chairs at bare wooden tables, drinking beer. Chev's best friend, Louie, was one of a core group of Tasso regulars. Even if Chev had not yet shown up, I could always count on finding Louie with his pale, strawberry-haired girlfriend Sandy molded to his side at a table in the center of the room.

One Saturday Louie, Chev, and a couple of other guys and their girlfriends drove to the country for a picnic. I don't remember why I did not join them. That night Chev burst through the front door, breathing heavily. "We had a flat tire on one of the back roads," he said. "While Louie was changing it, Sandy went for a walk. Then we heard this unbelievable screech and a thump. By the time we got there, Sandy was already dead."

Poof. Gone. Just like that. I could not believe it. Was this the kind of thing my father meant about getting hurt? Sandy didn't die because her boyfriend was black. And what role did I play in Sandy's death? If I had gone on the picnic, the molecules would have been rearranged, the timing different, and Sandy wouldn't have died. Maybe I would have gone on a walk and died.

A few days later, Louie flew to the Midwest to attend Sandy's funeral. I wondered how her parents felt when he showed up and whether they blamed him.

My roommates were not much more in favor of my palling around with Chev than my father was, and they would not allow him to move in. Instead, in the back of my VW we kept a roll of blankets and a couple of pillows. On the nights we stayed together, Chev and I drove to the tip of Hains Point where we slept on a spit of the nation's capital, embraced on three sides by the Potomac until daybreak. Part of the thrill was the forbiddenness of being there, and of being together.

Sometimes Chev preyed on my greatest vulnerability, my jealousy. One night on our bed by the water he told me, "I met a phat chick yesterday." I wasn't sure what that meant, but I knew it did not mean fat. I feigned a sulk, then we giggled and burrowed under the covers. That night in the curve of the river's smile we made love. While the rest of Washington was awash in sweat, the freedom of the night air cast a spell on us, fanning our faces with river breezes. We fell asleep giddy and awoke on our island of blankets, surrounded by damp, early morning grass, still laughing.

One of Chev's periods of absence extended into forever and our relationship just faded away. It must have been before the cold weather set in, because we never slept out in winter. A few weeks after I realized it was over, I read in the Washington Post that a couple had been murdered by the river, right where we had often slept.

Even though Chev and I had broken up, the freeze with my father continued. One afternoon, while driving to Dr. Woodward's office, I was so absorbed in my favorite death fantasy—the part at my funeral where sobbing Aunt Minnie consoles my heartbroken parents—that I swerved onto the exit ramp from the Beltway a second too late, mashing up the front right quadrant of my car. When I called my mom to ask how to file an insurance claim, she said, "Why don't you call Daddy and ask him?"

Feeling tentative but glad for the opportunity, I phoned my father that night. Except for the sensation of eggshells crumbling in my stomach, the conversation felt oddly normal, as though the past year had never happened. No mention of our estrangement or of Chev was ever made again by either of us.

Not long after Chev and I broke up, Dr. Woodward told me, "You don't need to come anymore, Susan."

I did not think therapists ever graduated their patients. Had I performed so well that she was breaking up with me? She invited me to visit her home the following week. On the one-hour drive from Washington, I wondered what to expect, other than being introduced to a barnyard of animals.

In Dr. Woodward's office I had always been brimming with chitchat, but sitting beside my psychiatrist in her cavernous living room—photographs eyeing me from pewter frames—my mind went blank the way it did with new boyfriends at the exact moments I wanted to be most charming. She asked whether I had any trips coming up, so I told her about a vacation I was planning to Jamaica where I hoped to meet Chev's mother, even though he and I were now just friends.

I did not volunteer any emotions. After all, I had been dismissed from therapy. As I rose to leave, she led me to the door, then paused. "Jim and I are retiring. We'll be selling the farm and moving to Maine," she said. "I want the isolation, and he wants to pan for gold. If you need anything you can phone Trish." Trish was her secretary who, by the way, was married to a black man. Why did we require Trish as a link to our relationship? Maybe I wasn't her surrogate daughter after all. Maybe Trish was.

A month later, I started thinking that maybe I had not really earned my independence from therapy, that perhaps it had simply been a convenient way for Dr. Woodward to release me, since she knew she was retiring. Then I reconsidered; she never would have lied to me. When I tried to call Trish at the office, the phone had already been disconnected. Another parental rejection, I thought. Then I worried that Dr.

Woodward must be dying of cancer and did not want to upset me, so she fabricated the Maine story. Why else would she disappear from my life like that, so abruptly and with such finality? For years it was hard to accept that I would never see her again; we had so much catching up to do.

ROUND EYE IN CHINA

"I Can't Go Through With It"
1977–1979

I had the most awful cold and was tempted to stay home. Yet I worried I might miss the chance to meet an intriguing stranger. It had been months since I'd been attracted to someone, so I blew my nose and headed into the autumn chill to go to a party.

I planted myself beside a table holding large bowls of pretzels and chips. That might sound like a tactic a shy person would use to avoid mingling, but I liked meeting new people. I just found it hard to settle in elsewhere if food was in a room. My zippy metabolism kept me slender.

My hand was on its way from the chips bowl to my mouth when a guy with warm, chestnut eyes approached. We exchanged names (his was Jeff) and chitchat, including that he was a lawyer at the State Department and that I was a stockbroker downtown.

I also wove in that I had taught math at a city college and that I had met our host at the Georgetown Flea Market, where on Sundays I sold my watercolors. "The kind of cutesy art people hang in their bathrooms," I said.

Jeff shared that he spoke Mandarin and had had a gig on a soap opera in Taiwan during the year he spent there between college and law school. We exchanged business cards. Although he was nice-looking and pleasant, I usually went for someone with more edge, someone noisier, more likely to be the center of attention. I am not sure why that was, since I liked to be the one in the spotlight. Typically if I met a group of guys, say on a ski slope, I would zoom in on the loudmouth, date him for a while, and allow him to overshadow whatever sparkle I had. Maybe that explained why I had not yet found Mr. Right.

A week later Jeff phoned to invite me to brunch the following afternoon at his apartment in Georgetown, which turned out to be around the corner from my apartment. "I'll make French toast," he said. Part of me thought, *It would be nice to go out instead,* and another part reflected, *This feels quaintly refreshing.*

Jeff lived on the second floor of a small brick townhouse that had been converted to a duplex. The cozy living room with off-white walls and pale gray carpet felt as welcoming as my childhood home.

"My father taught me how to make this," Jeff said in the tiny kitchen, as he dipped Wonder Bread into an egg mixture." Within minutes I scarfed down two pieces of French toast. Now what? I felt awkward, anxious to learn more about him, not ready for physical contact.

Jeff suggested a walk. As we strolled along cobblestone streets, past eighteenth-century townhouses and mansions the color of butter, he asked, "What's it like being a stockbroker?"

"It helps to know the markets, but it's a lot about selling. I love closing a sale," I answered, musing to myself how hard it was not to think of him or anyone with a buck in his pocket as a prospective client. I added that during my first full year I had ranked second in all of Merrill Lynch for opening new accounts. I immediately regretted boasting, so I tried to offset that by telling him how I froze the first time my boss ordered me to pick up the phone and sell a stock.

Jeff emitted, "Uh huh." *He's not all that fascinated,* I thought. I asked about his work at the State Department. He named places under his jurisdiction that I had never heard of, like the Solomon Islands. "Uh huh," I said.

We had been walking for over an hour when Jeff asked if I wanted to see his costume for a Halloween party that night. Back at his place, the sweet French toast aroma lingered. While Jeff changed, I perused titles on a bookshelf, most of which related to China. It would be difficult to overstate how little this interested me.

Jeff emerged from his bedroom wearing flippers, goggles, a snorkel, and a burgundy bathrobe with sponges pinned all over. I was glad he didn't—as I would—allow vanity to get in the way of looking ridiculous. I laughed and praised his creativity. In the final light of the day, he stood there waving good-bye, his flippered feet forming a wide vee. I felt cautiously hopeful.

The following week, I phoned Jeff to ask if he wanted to meet me after work at the Kennedy Center to see the screwball comedy *It Happened One Night*. I sensed he wasn't enthusiastic about the film but he said yes, the same way—in the beginning of relationships—I agreed to go places in which I had little interest.

Jeff arrived looking pleasingly professional in a peach-colored shirt and a tan tweed suit. I liked that he would wear a peach shirt; this was a secure guy.

After the movie, we stopped at a bistro to share a quarter chicken. I snatched the wing, so he could have the plump, juicy breast meat. On the walk home, he told me the wing was his favorite chicken part. I confessed the breast was mine. When would I learn that not everyone took in the world as I did? We kissed goodnight at my door.

The following week I read about a Toastmasters speech competition and told Jeff about it. The night we were to go, I skipped down the steps behind my apartment building that linked my block to the small side street he lived on. Shortly after I mounted the stairs to his duplex, we began making out and never made it to Toastmasters. We spent the rest of the night in his bed. Between bouts of passion, we exchanged pillow talk of past relationships. In contrast to me, his former girlfriends had been either blonde or Chinese.

Jeff had dark, good looks with delicate features. His mother was French and bought all his clothes. In hospitals people thought he was a doctor. I thought he looked like Alan Alda. My mother thought he looked like me. My friend Hope said he had sad eyes.

We may have looked alike and we fit together size-wise— my five feet five to his five feet nine—but we were hardly similar. Jeff had a global perspective; I knew the neighborhood. In Chinese restaurants, he ordered in Mandarin; my verbal skills included the ability to say words backwards. Neither of us was as impressed with the other's linguistic talents as we each thought the other ought to be. I had strong likes and dislikes and communicated them with vim. Jeff's narrow range of expression, from "not bad" to "I'd rather not," took getting used to.

I told Hope, "Sometimes I want to shake him to get a reaction."

Yet Jeff was gentle and affectionate. One day he said, "You need a nickname." With other boyfriends, such monikers sprung up naturally. Jeff said he had called a former sweetheart "Sweetie," so that was out for me. And his most recent girlfriend—the one whose Flex shampoo I used because it was still in his shower—he had called "Noodle." He decided I would be "Cutie" and called me "Q" for short, a nickname for my nickname.

He was not a Honey or a Darling, so I called him Jeffie, which was what his family called him. Was it a sign that I had little inspiration to come up with a pet name for him?

Much of our intimacy came from nonverbal closeness, such as the showers we took together and the winter nights we fell asleep on the floor, entwined in layers of worn quilts by a fire in his living room, a Judy Collins LP spinning on his stereo.

In addition to a strong physical attraction, it's hard to say exactly what drew me to Jeff. He was certainly bright and his agreeableness made him easy to get along with. Too easy, perhaps. His interest in government began to stimulate an awareness in me. And I must also not underestimate the effect of displays of affection. Feeling loved by someone had the power to trigger a loving response. When I was in his arms, pressed against his soft, cashmere crew neck, any reservations I had about him dissolved. This felt like a place I belonged.

Yet I did not feel as much rapport with Jeff as I had experienced a few years earlier with a beau named Elliott. Elliott and I had spent hours devouring each other in conversation along with the pasta dinners we made in his mini apartment, which was not unlike Jeff's, except Elliott alphabetized his fridge food (apple sauce, baba ganoush, . . .). I loved Elliott's quirks. What were Jeff's quirks, other than his attraction to China, which few others had at that time? Wasn't that more of a career path than a quirk?

Like me, Elliott could talk backwards. And we both loved camping, although his outdoor equipment could fill the trunk of his white Mustang convertible trunk, while I owned a sleeping bag. On our first camping trip together he was pitching his oversized tent, and I was trying to figure out how to hang a bag with my aspirins so the bears couldn't get to them when, all of a sudden, we heard a trash can rattling. It was a bear! I was so terrified that Elliott said we could pack up and find a room somewhere. That was the moment I fell in love with him. The problem was that a long-term girlfriend named Susan Fishman was not part of Elliott's plan. When he moved to New York, he declined my request to join him.

A year and a half into my relationship with Jeff, he asked, "How would you feel about moving to Hong Kong?"

He was hatching an idea to work in a law office there. I visualized neon "Chop Suey" signs. He knew how uninformed I was, so he picked up a globe from the corner of his bedroom and pointed to a small, pink amoebic shape on the other side of the world.

I was an adrenaline junkie, but not the kind to yo-yo on a bungee jump if they'd had bungee jumps. I could get a fix just by cutting the timing close when meeting a friend for dinner. A way better rush resulted from life change, especially one like moving to the far-off, little pink amoeba.

Jeff had not mentioned marriage as part of the Hong Kong

plan, but this seemed like the right time for us to say "I do" or break up. I was thirty-three years old and wanted kids. Jeff was twenty-nine and wanted kids someday. One of the things I worried about most was regret, so I was not going to allow the opportunity to bear children pass.

Having children, like dropping letters in mailboxes, was one of life's few unalterable actions; marriages, of course, could come and go. So a few years earlier I had said to myself, *I need to decide if I want kids.* And then I said to myself, *Yes.* With a husband seemed like a good idea.

This was April and I gave Jeff a marriage ultimatum that included a commitment to have children. In June, he was to opt in or out.

June rolled around and Jeff waited until the moment my ultimatum was about to expire before agreeing to marry, which promptly catapulted him deep into what he called "the black hole." In the hole, Jeff became glum and uncommunicative. So we went to a psychiatrist. Was there a message here: two husbands-to-be, two premarital therapy visits?

Jeff did most of the talking while I suppressed my own uncertainties about getting hitched to someone so reluctant to commit. Despite his lack of enthusiasm, I bought our wedding rings and had mine engraved with *Love always, Jeff.*

Several weeks later Jeff and I were in bed watching television. Four days remained until more than a hundred friends and relatives were to witness our exchange of vows. Jeff shut off the TV and turned to me looking all sad and serious and said, "I can't go through with it." I felt as though a monstrous, hairy hand had reached inside me and was squeezing my intestines. Since we had already masticated this getting married issue to a colorless pulp, I simply did not know what else to do but to start uninviting.

Plus I thought, *If I begin phoning people to tell them I'm canceling the wedding, he might realize his mistake.* The first person I dialed was my mother, who told me she understood and assured me I would be fine. Early the following day she headed downtown to return the dress she had bought for the occasion.

Next I phoned my friend Arthur, who responded, "I never liked him anyway." Oops for Arthur since, after I came back from a teary night at a friend's apartment, my flip-flopping fiancé said we should marry after all.

What a cliffhanger our impending union had become. In a deep subcutaneous core, what doubts did I harbor? Was anyone ever a hundred per cent positive? If Jeff could keep his balance for just a few more days, then I was not going to poke around my own gut and risk bumping into a voice directing me to reverse the plans we had made to marry and move to Asia.

It was not until a few hours before Jeff and I were to stand beneath a chuppa on the Hotel Washington's rooftop—facing blue sky, Jimmy Carter's White House, and Rabbi Gordon, whom I had found in the Yellow Pages—that I believed for certain our marriage would occur. In a spacious suite provided by the hotel, I sat on a beige silk ottoman, wearing my new champagne-colored, one-piece undergarment, while my friend Sue blow-dried my hair with long strokes of a brush.

Jeff, meanwhile, sat wearing a pale blue polo shirt in a restaurant several floors below, sharing a turkey sandwich with his former law professor. Unbeknownst to me, professor and protégé agreed that, rather than Hong Kong, we would all move to Peking where the two of them would counsel clients for an international law firm. Jeff figured correctly that I would relish the switch to this exotic destination. Before changing into his suit, he told me the news. He was as exuberant as I had ever seen him at the prospect of finally going to the People's Republic of China and establishing the first post-normalization law presence there.

The following day, on our flight to London for a brief honeymoon, I began studying Mandarin from Jeff's old college textbook.

ONE-MINUTE HISTORY OF CHINA
1958 - 1976

In 1958 Mao Tse-tung (later known as Mao Zedong) initiated the Great Leap Forward, which lasted until 1960. During that period, factories replaced fertile rice fields and twenty million people starved to death. Then, in 1966, the Cultural Revolution began; Mao's intention was to wipe out poverty and class differences. He ordered schools closed and intellectuals sent to the countryside for "re-education." Some scholars and landlords were humiliated, forced to march around town centers in dunce caps. Others were tortured or killed. Schools shut down, books were burned, and art destroyed, along with millions of lives. For ten years, teenage Red Guards reigned over chaos and violence, even denouncing their own parents in the name of communism.

Flash Forward: I Spy A Spy
2007

It was 1979, during the aftermath of the Cultural Revolution, when Jeff and I first landed in Peking. Throughout the eighties we went back often. And then, after a long hiatus, I returned in 2007 for a nostalgic visit to what was now called Beijing.

From my jumbo jet window, the flat landscape surrounding Beijing Capital International Airport still looked like a massive vacant lot. After riding in a thicket of traffic, I strode from my taxi to the reception desk of the Ascott Hotel, trying to absorb the opulence, polite service, and cleanliness that had been unimaginable in the Communist China I remembered.

I dropped my bags in the room, grabbed my helmet, and headed straight to a bicycle shop. The equivalent of forty dollars bought me a shiny black Flying Pigeon with lock, bell, and metal basket. Although I was impatient to check out the new and unfamiliar, I was even more eager to uncover the old and recognizable, the city I encountered when I touched down in 1979 to live here with Jeff.

Pedaling along a narrow road, lined with little shops, it was as though I had returned to a stage set where I had performed a generation earlier. Characters came into view, dressed in colorful sweaters and pants or swishy skirts—similar to what people wore at home in Washington. Such fashions were unheard of for Chinese in the late seventies, when it would come as a sweet surprise just to see a snippet of a red knitted cardigan peek out from under the high, squared neckline of a young woman's olive drab Mao uniform.

Blaring horns: familiar. Bumper-to-bumper cars: unfamiliar. The ratio of cars to bicycles had flip-flopped. In every direction, steel frames of soon-to-be buildings rose from the earth, crisscrossed with bamboo scaffolding.

Had I not anticipated the profusion of construction and motor vehicles, I would have felt violated; instead I felt loss, not only of the Peking I had known, but also of the life I'd had nearly thirty years earlier, with a future full of surprises. I decided that the following day I would pedal to the Peking Hotel, now called the Beijing Hotel, where Jeff and I lived for fifteen months in the period before cranes dangling this way and that—like rickety stairways to heaven—created a whole new skyline.

The next morning I awakened to one of those Beijing skies that suggested it was either about to sprinkle or that the sun was simply masked behind a blanket of smog. I stuffed a rain jacket into my bike basket and headed west on Chang'an Avenue. It was intoxicating to know my way around. Even with all that had changed, both in China and in my life, familiarity embraced me.

A revolving door at the Beijing Hotel's side entrance featured a plastic flower arrangement, as tall as I was, sealed between two of the glass partitions. This floral touch was new, but its kitschiness evoked my old China. Just inside, Outback Steakhouse beckoned, and after less than one day, I felt so at home—without the pressure a tourist might have experienced to seek indigenous nourishment—that I allowed my American appetite to lead me into Outback for a salad and a baked Idaho. Oh, what I would have given for a bowl of greens like this, back when there were no foreign chains and when eating uncooked vegetables in this unsanitary city was the health-risk equivalent of ingesting pork tartare.

It took as long as a leisurely cup of tea to walk from one end of the Beijing Hotel to the other. I couldn't help noticing what was missing: the cafe that provided Peking's nightlife, where we often sat after dinner, sipping coffee that tasted like Postum, chatting with whoever passed by—journalists, Bloomingdale's CEO, diplomats, Seiji Ozawa; the barbershop—with a price list for each body part, like arms for the equivalent of a dollar thirty-five—where nearly every day I spent a half hour settled into a raised chair while Madame Chen covered me with a silk sheet and then worked her thumbs into my knotted muscles; the post office where, for one of my countless collections, I bought new issues of stamps featuring Peking opera faces and grinning pigtailed girls on tractors; the counter where they sold coveted international goods—our lifelines to the rest of the world—*Newsweek, Time, The International Herald Tribune,* M&Ms; the Chinese medicine shop, really just another counter, where they sold potions made from Chinese mountain ants and deer antlers—some promised long life and one, made from bees, cured my persistent cough.

That hall, with a ceiling so high it could have been the sky, was my village, my downtown, my mall, if I had been one to frequent a mall. Circumstances had improved drastically for Beijing residents, only a privileged few of whom were even permitted to pass through the automatic sliding glass doors of this mega-structure in 1979. But a selfish part of me longed for the way things had been.

Toward the end of my stroll through memory lane, I paused near a wide, red-carpeted stairway where a signboard heralded Beijing International Fashion Week and listed a schedule of runway events. A show of young designers was soon to begin. At a nearby counter, where a rainbow of neatly folded silk scarves fanned out on its glass shelves, I asked a young saleswoman how I could get a ticket. She replied with a phrase I remembered well, "*Mei you ban fa*," meaning "no way." Just then, an older man wearing a white hotel uniform sidled up to me and asked in English, "Didn't you live here in 1980?"

Whoa. How did he know that? With a mix of English and Mandarin, he said that back then he worked in the hotel flower shop. He remembered the red wooden earrings made in Mexico that I wore all the time. And that my lawyer husband spoke good Chinese and that I went back to the States, had a baby there in 1982, and looked fat when I returned to China a year and a half later. And that during the Gang of Four trial I said I would be *shufu*, which means comfortable, if the defendants were executed. He was right on all counts.

I would have hardly felt more exposed if the flower man had just undressed me. Plus, I didn't even remember a flower shop. What else did he know? I complimented his memory and then asked if he could get me into the fashion show. He pulled out his cell phone and dialed his friend, who happened to be a security guard. "It is all fixed," he said and I smiled, both for "the fix" and for my high expectations for the show.

The flower man steered me away from the red stairway to a back door, which was a perfect metaphor, because—as in English—going through the "back door" or *hou men* was the Chinese expression for wangling something you could not obtain by going through, say, the front door. Going through the back door had been so common that it was my *modus operandi*, including securing permission from the authorities to adopt in 1986 before China was set up for foreign adoptions.

It wasn't until the following night at dinner with my old friend Xiao Hu, Jeff's former driver, that I began to wonder whether the flower man had been my very own spy. In the late seventies, most expatriate foreigners were aware of being watched—everyone had a story—but it had never occurred to me that the snooping might have been so personalized. One American, who lived in the hotel back then, told me about the time he dialed a number and heard a recording of his own voice from a previous conversation. The "listener" apparently had hit "play" rather than "record."

I reported the flower man encounter to Xiao Hu, who had always known the workings of the hotel. He confirmed my suspicions, which got me wondering whether Xiao Hu himself—now the manager of an artificial Christmas tree factory outside of Beijing—had also been a spy when we first knew him.

In this new, fashion-show China, my former spy had become my benefactor. Never having been to a fashion show, I anticipated movie stars and editors of glossy magazines. I was dressed in a navy blue V-neck and jeans with a Velcro strap around my pants leg to keep it from catching in my bicycle chain. The stadium-type seating was so jammed with ordinary

Chinese yuppies that I had to sit on a step, my red backpack wedged between my feet. With heads blocking my view, I stood up in order to see each time the audience applauded for couture draped on a chopstick-thin, arch-backed model sashaying down the runway.

I had been in China's twelve-hours-later time zone for only one day, and soon I felt weary from all the popping up, so I just stayed down. Amid everyone's legs, my eyes focused on all the high heels and men's leather shoes.

If this had been 1979, much of the footwear would have been black canvas slip-ons with thin white rubber soles. Then again if this had been 1979, there would have been no fashion show. Back then you could barely make out a person's gender, other than that of those women whose pigtails poked down from under their caps. The masses wore baggy pants and Mao jackets, usually made from green or blue heavy cotton that looked limp, as though having endured dozens—if not hundreds—of washings. Government officials dressed in the Mao style too. However, their garments tended to be flawlessly tailored, often in a gray material that looked like wool but was more likely to have been polyester, which had had more cachet than natural fibers.

The ubiquitous Mao suits were the first things that trumpeted China's staggering uniformity when I arrived in 1979 Peking as a newly married thirty-three-year-old, who had left career, friends, condo, and VW convertible in Washington, D.C. to embark on the unknown with my groom.

Sex for Three:
Communist-Style

1979

Two weeks after we married, Jeff and I eased into our long, rust-stained bathtub in the old wing of the Peking Hotel, less than a mile from the Forbidden City. Sitting armpit-deep and foot-to-foot with him in the warm water, I leaned forward and whispered, "Do you think they're listening?" It was our first night in Communist China. We would soon learn from other foreigners that the cryptic seventeenth floor of the new wing, where the elevator never stopped, was indeed the listening department.

We continued our bath in hushed tones, agreeing to explore the city if we woke early enough. I asked Jeff if he thought we'd be followed.

Thrilled by the prospect, I envisioned men in round cotton caps, blue Mao suits, and black cloth shoes peering at us through monocles from behind lampposts.

The bathwater relaxed me, though I was still reeling a bit

from the mini-drama involving my cross-country skis that had unfolded a few hours earlier.

After the twenty-six hour trip with a four-hour layover in Tokyo's spotless airport, everything in Peking's air terminal had looked drab and lifeless. People moved at a pace that suggested they had no particular place to go. It was like being in a black and white movie in slow motion, especially compared to my Technicolor life as a stockbroker back in Washington. Nonetheless, flutters coursed through my body from the unfamiliarity of it all and from the suspense of what lay ahead.

I had exited customs behind Jeff, pushing a wobbly cart stacked so high with luggage that I had to reach with one arm to keep them from toppling, while stretching the rest of me to see where I was headed. Lao Wang and Xiao Sun, eager representatives of our host organization, greeted us with wide grins and took charge of our carts with great enthusiasm.

Sun followed behind Wang, whose round face bore a resemblance to the framed pictures of Chairman Mao that hung inside the airport and already felt omnipresent. They led us to a white minibus and began loading our eighteen mismatched suitcases (mostly mine) as well as a pair of boxed, twelve-speed bicycles and my cross-country skis. My father-in-law, a geography professor, had waged a losing argument against my taking skis, saying Peking had barely any precipitation, let alone snow. To me, a single snow shower with one-inch accumulation would have made it worthwhile.

In the airport's parking lot, Jeff, trying to be helpful, slid my skis sideways across the back seat. They didn't quite wedge in and he kept coaxing them, a bit too vigorously, shattering a window and, along with it, his first moments on Chinese soil. My stomach flipped with guilt, and more so, with fear of Jeff being irate.

Jeff's eyes widened and his rare but characteristic display of extreme disapproval—fists clenched, temples pulsing—began. As we stood in the chilly evening air, Wang and Sun rattled off a string of Chinese words to each other. Sun gestured with a basketball-dribbling motion to reassure us. Wang, who spoke some English, said, "It is no problem. We shall fix the window tomorrow."

As we drove along a road lined with barren trees, Sun kept turning from the front seat to say something in Mandarin. Jeff, whose language skills were part of the deal, confided softly to me with a troubled brow, "I'm having a hard time understanding him." I was relieved that my husband had bigger things to worry about than the glass he had broken with my skis.

We turned onto Chang An Avenue, the widest boulevard I had ever seen. Somewhere I heard it had been designed this wide to allow an ox cart to make a U-turn. In fact I saw some animal-drawn carts and hardly any motor vehicles. By contrast, the bike lanes—one on each far side—were dense with cyclists, streams of blues and greens under lit street lamps that resembled clusters of round white balloons against the black autumn sky.

A crowd of gawkers lined the curved driveway to the Peking Hotel, where two men in army uniforms stood at attention. Proportionate to the communist-scale giganticness of the boulevard in front, the building ended way in the distance. Wide, glass doors parted and I stepped inside to a conspicuous display of red, China's most auspicious color, symbolizing luck and happiness as well as revolution, all of which would play a role in my future with Jeff.

On a sea of plush cherry carpeting in the brightly-lit lobby, a young fellow wearing a gray Mao jacket that hung loosely over his slouched shoulders stopped us and impassively examined our passports before allowing us to proceed.

That first night in China, worried about the spies, we had sex as quietly as if my mother were awake in an adjoining room. I then slept in jet-lagged spurts until six a.m., which was six p.m. back home. I awoke hungry for dinner.

HIGH LOW
1979

Jeff awoke with a hunger as ravenous as mine, so we dressed quickly and went to the dining room on the main floor, my first and only Chinese buffet breakfast. In a blue and white porcelain bowl, I placed one spoonful of rice gruel and a steamed bun. I passed over the shiny mushrooms and greens that were floating in a translucent, gelatinous liquid.

After breakfast we met up with our bags in our permanent quarters in the newest wing of the hotel. Inside our room on the tenth floor, just down the hall from Jeff's office, I pushed a button that drew apart the orange drapes. We stopped puzzling over the oddity of electric curtains when the thrilling bustle along Chang An Avenue unfolded below; from above light poured in, given the southern exposure and expanse of blue sky.

Despite incessant horn-honking from the few cars on the avenue, Jeff closed his eyes with a contented sigh, peaceful as a curled-up puppy in the warmth of interior sunlight. Here was

China, Jeff's dream, right under our noses!

There was only one problem. I simply could not erase from my mind a scenario in which rescuers' ladders would be too short to reach us on the tenth floor in the event of a fire.

After several minutes, I worked up the nerve to tell Jeff how anxious I felt, and he reluctantly agreed that I could request a move to a lower level. I loved him extra for that.

So while he was at work I helped the *fuwuyuan* or "room boys," who populated each floor of the hotel, schlep our twelve bags down to room 5040 on the fifth floor, which—although half as high—made me only ten percent less queasy. We would still die if we had to jump. The decor was identical to that of the previous room, what you would have called modern if this had been 1950: twin beds, a pair of upholstered chairs covered in orange duck cloth that flanked a blond wooden table, and a door leading to a (*gulp*) balcony. A desk, thick navy carpet, and blond wooden closet doors completed the look. The white-tiled bathroom was large enough to accommodate a green chair, which stood beside a tub that featured only a hand shower.

When Jeff returned, I imagined he would be pleased that I had unpacked nearly all of our clothes, toiletries, and books, though the thought that he might be displeased with the dreary view and northern exposure must have taken a little junket around my cerebellum. What I had not anticipated was that his reaction to the new digs would make his pulsing and clenching after the window-broken-by-skis incident seem like a celebration.

Without looking at me, Jeff strode across the room. For a long while, he gazed out the window and across the alley at the gray, nondescript building that filled our view. Then he kicked the radiator and turned to face me. My skin went icy.

In the two years I had known Jeff, I had never witnessed anything like the radiator kick. I recognized that for anyone else this kick, as a physical expression of displeasure, might be a small gesture; a less gentle soul would have kicked me. But given that the kicker was Jeff, to whom outward displays of anger were unseemly, it was a big deal. The way his lips pursed and his eyes seared a hole right through me, I immediately thought, *Okay, Jeff will not recover from this. Our marriage is over.* It may sound counterintuitive, but imagining the worst helped me to calm down.

My reaction to Jeff's reaction revealed less about Jeff than about my all-or-nothing thinking, my literal way of taking in the world without a great deal of processing. Add to that my dread of other people's anger, dating back to my father's booming voice when provoked and all the provoking I had done.

One good thing about Jeff was that he did not stay angry. When something really displeased him, he reacted with a mini implosion and then made a leap. Typically he shrugged and said, "Oh well." This time, though, he went all quiet. Thankfully, we had dinner plans with a journalist acquaintance.

Jeff's complete rebound took longer than usual, yet by the following morning a remarkable reversal had taken place. Above all else Jeff liked to sleep in a dark, quiet room. After a night of delicious slumber in 5040 in the shadow of the drab building across the way and with no cacophony of horns, he was practically thanking me. In fact, he pointed out that he still had the Chang An Avenue view from his office, though the sun made the suite where he worked so hot that they had to keep the curtains closed.

And so began my life in Peking.

ROUND EYE IN PEKING
1979–1981

I was eager to take on everything at once: get the bikes we had brought from home assembled, learn Mandarin, and find something more purposeful to do besides cycling around the city and practicing my primitive language skills on shop girls. Not that I ever would have grown weary of that.

Learning Chinese was my top priority. With Jeff as my spokesperson, I felt trapped in a silent film, or at least a film in which I was silenced. One afternoon I wandered into a restaurant alone. In the front room, crammed with the masses, I pointed to an empty chair and the manager shook his head and waved his hand from side to side. Frustrated and with no other means to communicate, I stomped my foot like a spoiled child. I wanted to mingle with the *laobaixing*, the ordinary people, rather than sit behind a curtain in one of the private rooms reserved for foreigners. Most days I sat on a park bench for lunch, eating oranges and nuts, and in winter, steaming sweet potatoes served from smoky black drums.

Finally Jeff and I went to a restaurant where—in a calm, soft tone—he talked the manager into letting us eat in the main section. At circular tables practically tangent to one another, seats were filled with men in blue suits and caps, slurping noodle soup or chewing on chicken parts and then spitting the bones on the floor. Nearly everyone in Peking seemed to have upper respiratory conditions, and some of our tablemates were coughing and spitting globs of mucous on the floor. We slurped our own bowls of dumpling soup and paid the roughly thirty-three-cent bill. Subsequently, I decided, I would seek cultural immersion elsewhere.

Frequently after dinner Jeff and I went for a walk. On one such stroll, Jeff pointed out that with so few white people in Peking, no matter what we did, the Chinese thought it was typical behavior of the "round eye" or "big nose," as Caucasians were sometimes referred to. Simultaneously, to prove the point, we broke into a Mexican hat dance in the middle of the sidewalk, jumping from foot to foot with hands on hips then linking arms and spinning around. The stares we drew were neither greater in number nor different from the ones we got when just sauntering down the street.

Sometimes before bed we ambled along a path I dubbed Lovers Lane. It was a tree-lined strip near the hotel, flanked by a narrow road on each side. Given that many Chinese lived with multiple generations sharing only a couple of rooms, the nighttime darkness on Lovers Lane provided couples, even married ones, with welcome privacy. Whenever we walked in unlit areas, we saw silhouettes of embracing pairs in the shadows: behind bushes, against walls, or on secluded benches.

Our own spots for stolen kisses, not that we needed any,

were empty elevators in the Peking Hotel. If we found ourselves alone, I'd push the button for our floor, and then Jeff
would press against me on the side of the car and I'd wrap my
arms around his neck. Our marriage felt so right.

Jeff and I now ordered yogurt and pancakes for breakfast
from room service. To keep us informed, the hotel provided
a daily copy of the English-language *Xinhua*, literally "new
speech," which was a stapled, Xerox summary of news from
around the world. Well, to call it news is an overstatement,
given headlines such as, "Traffic Jam in Chad." One article explained a Peking insect-killing drive: in an effort to "restore
the city's reputation as a 'flyless city' as in the 1950s . . . thousands upon thousands of pupils armed with fly-swatters have
been waging the fight against flies and mosquitos [sic]."

News from home was more difficult. A month after we
arrived, sixty-six Americans were taken hostage at the U.S.
Embassy in Iran. The time in captivity for fifty-two of them
lasted nearly as long as our fifteen months in Peking. Every
day we listened to *Voice of America*, hoping for their release.
Instead, one morning we awoke to the news that John Lennon
had been shot dead.

The most jarring news from home arrived in a letter
from my parents that included a two-page spread in *The
Philadelphia Inquirer*. Two of my high school classmates had
been carried away by a riptide off the coast of Mexico. Lost
at sea. Presumed dead. This kind of news was devastating to
hear anywhere, but receiving it so many time zones away from
home added a layer of grief. These reports of disaster became
frequent visitors to my thoughts. I'd had a lifetime of practice,
able to remember every tragedy I had ever heard about, as
though by collecting these catastrophes I could perform the

magical thinking trick of preventing them from happening to me.

At last, through the Diplomatic Services Bureau, Xiao Sun arranged a tutor for me. Everything had to go through channels.

Enter Mr. Yin, who showed up on a Monday morning at precisely nine o'clock for my first Mandarin lesson. I welcomed him into my room by placing some loose tea in a porcelain cup and pouring steaming water over it, releasing the fragrant aroma of jasmine. Teacher Yin smiled and his eyes seemed to close behind his black-rimmed glasses. Was he forty? Fifty? It was hard to tell; his skin was the color of rubber bands and equally smooth. He was about my height and wore a dark-gray Mao suit with the most impeccable fit. His black lace-up shoes were polished to a high shine. Honestly, he looked fine enough to dance at the White House.

I told Mr. Yin that I had been a stockbroker, which he taught me to say in Mandarin: *mai mai gupiao*, literally "buy sell stock." Clearly it was not a financial consultant who came up with the idea for *mai* to be the Mandarin sound for both "buy" and "sell," with only tones to distinguish them. I tried to imagine the confusion if a tone-deaf individual (like me) were to try trading financial securities in Chinese.

I shared with Mr. Yin what it was like during the three years I had worked at a Merrill Lynch office in D.C., where I made fifty phone calls a day to strangers. Whenever I wasn't on the phone, my job was like being at a party, I said, because I sat in a room with forty-seven other brokers, mostly men, and the guys around me were always yukking it up. I liked spiking my English with colloquialisms that I could teach my teacher. After several months we began conversing only in Mandarin, though I never did master the tones, so who knows what he thought I was saying.

Similar to how I tried to entertain my psychiatrists, I liked making Mr. Yin laugh. During the first of several modest snowfalls that year, I skied in Tiananmen Square, and when I told Mr. Yin about all the stares I drew, he chuckled like a bemused grandfather.

After my lesson, I would turn on my boom box until lunchtime and play audiotapes I had brought from home: *My Fair Lady, The King and I, Fiddler on the Roof.* I played them over and over while absorbing all I could from my Mandarin grammar book.

My text doubled as a communist handbook with vocabulary like *tongzhi,* which means comrade, and *ziligengsheng,* meaning self-reliance—specifically, regeneration through one's own efforts—a definition that went way beyond how my mother had used "self-reliance" when she wanted me to clean my room. As I studied, the Mandarin in my head merged with the show tunes in the air to form a delicious blend of East and West, Old World and new.

Sometimes I went downstairs for lunch in the Peking Hotel dining room, which was immortalized in a December, 1979 front-page *Wall Street Journal* article as being "abuzz at every meal with foreign businessmen discussing the deals they are after . . ." It was especially abuzz at the noon hour.

Most Chinese people smiled readily, as though life had treated them well, which it had not. Rather, they had learned to *chi ku,* literally "eat bitter," during the brutal decades under Mao. Among those who never smiled were the wait staff in the Peking Hotel dining room. You would wave to catch the attention of a waitress who was looking exactly your way, but who would cast her eyes just over your head, pretending not to see you. When finally she decided to take your order, she would shuffle over with baby steps. Then came the waiting for your food. Waiting was part of the communist experience. The *Wall Street Journal* article quoted the dining room's deputy manager: "We can't blame the young workers for their bad attitude. After all, they were taught during the Cultural Revolution that 'to rebel is right.'"

Sometimes, when I ate lunch in the hotel, I sat alone reading *Newsweek* even when Jeff was eating alone at another table, reading *Time*. I savored my own daytime space.

A useful word I learned during my first lesson with Mr. Yin was *cha*, which means tea. That afternoon, I ventured outside to practice my new sounds in nearby alleys called *hutongs*. No place in all of Peking was as charming as these lanes with their centuries of history.

A sense of mystery stemmed from the walls that blocked my view into courtyards of low houses that lined the narrow lanes. These one-story, pewter-colored courtyard homes with orange tile roofs often served as quarters to mother-in-law/daughter-in-law pairs who, it was popularly believed, loathed each other.

Socks, undershirts, and hankies dangled overhead, pinned onto lines strung across the *hutongs*, while rusty bicycles leaned against walls, along whose top edges the occasional scrawny cat crept. Birdcages hung on nails that protruded from the sides of buildings, and birdsong formed a chorus with the click clack of old men and women chattering and the steady jingle jangle of bicycle bells. On sloping tile rooftops orange peels, which residents used to treat indigestion and nausea, baked in the sun.

Other than bright splotches of color from children's clothing, the overall impression was gray, especially at dusk when coal smoke arose from courtyards signaling the pre-dinner bustle: bicyclists with bunches of large white cabbage leaves strapped to racks above their rear tires, a grandmother with one arm wrapped around a bare-bottomed baby and the other around a paper package of noodles, schoolchildren sitting on low stools under the light of streetlamps while writing in flimsy notebooks. Here and there a tiny shop brightened the landscape with a show of household products, such as lime- and cherry-colored rubber pails and enamel tin bowls—large enough to soak your feet in—with images of bloated orange goldfish.

Sugary scents from little stalls, which sold sticky balls of dough rolled in sesame seeds, blended with the acrid stench from rectangular structures the color of cigarette ashes that served as neighborhood men's and women's "toilets." These facilities housed gutters running the length of cement or dirt floors, which neighbors straddled while squatting, one behind the other. Well after dark, workers arrived on bicycles with huge containers for collecting the "night soil" that would be used as fertilizer, one reason it was a bad idea to eat raw vegetables. Even when I ate vegetables that were cooked, I had to block out images of how they had been cultivated.

The way a breadcrumb draws a clot of ants, I drew onlookers wherever I went. I stepped into a little shop, and a crowd followed me. When I asked for cha, my audience laughed, so I did too. I felt like a celebrity. I did not really want tea; I just wanted to try out the word. Given my inability to vocalize the rising second tone, or any of the four Mandarin tones, the woman behind the counter may have thought I was asking for a fork, a raft, a quarrel, a Buddhist monastery, or panties, to name a few things that sounded like cha.

My onlookers' laughter subsided and the shop girl replied reflexively, "*Mei you.*" I would come to learn that she did not mean that tea was out of stock. Rather the woman said "not have," because she did not want to make the effort to understand someone as foreign as I was. I exited the little shop, trailed by the group that had followed me in.

A pattern to my days emerged of studying Mandarin in my hotel room and then—from the saddle of my twelve-speed—navigating Peking as though it were a life-sized theme park.

I heard about the Canton Fair—it had a carnival ring—and I wanted to check it out. An equal draw was the thirty-three-hour train ride.

When I arrived at my bunk-bedded rail compartment, my three roommates were already in their pajamas. Two of the men, a father and grown son, sat snapping open sunflower seeds with their teeth. They both spoke a little English, yet I had the best rapport with the third man, Fan Dan—a long-haired journalist for a Hong Kong newspaper—who spoke no English. He and I communicated by gesturing and drawing pictures in a small notebook.

People often said how great it was to share experiences like this. But I learned the pleasures of traveling alone during my first trip to Europe, which I took with two college classmates. After spending the first three mornings waiting in a London bed and breakfast for my travel mates to curl their eyelashes, I ignored the meticulously crafted itinerary my father had insisted upon and took off on my own for Paris.

Ah, the freedom of roving around the Left Bank solo, sitting in a cafe all day with a glass of warm Coke if I wanted. I began to think in arithmetical terms about how it felt to shed my companions: three of us sharing the same adventures had made everything only one-third as marvelous.

The best part of being a singleton was the ease of talking to strangers. Language differences, rather than posing a barrier, gave me license to step over boundaries I might not have crossed at home. And I welcomed the freedom to go off with a Danish guy I met in a leather market.

Now that I was married to Jeff, having a fling with a wandering Dane was no longer an option. I was, however, free to engage in a most dazzling affair with this expansive, enigmatic landmass full of oddities, such as being all one time zone.

The Canton Fair was like a department store the size of a village with the gestalt of a boardwalk, offering every type of *chozzerai* (Yiddish for junk) manufactured in China. Canton the city now known as Guangzhou felt more relaxed than Peking with its warm climate and lush vegetation. In the parks clusters of old men played cards, while others congregated with their caged birds. Under a gazebo in a square, couples in Western-style clothing swing danced to strains of Louis Armstrong.

I'd had a splendid time. Then came the regret. I returned to Beijing to the unsettling news that Jeff had had an even better time. I wasn't competing; it's just that while I was off on my exotic jaunt, he was off on one even more exotic. If I had stayed in Peking, I would have gotten to travel with Jeff to Tientsin (now Tianjin) along with his client H. R. "Bob" Haldeman, Nixon's chief of staff who had spent eighteen months in jail for his participation in the Watergate scandal.

Haldeman wanted to convert a former retreat for Mao and other leaders into a hotel. Set in a park and completely walled-in, the retreat now accommodated guests of the government.

Had I been there, I would have slept beside my husband in what had formerly been Premier Zhou Enlai's bedroom. The only thing that soothed my disappointment was that Jeff and the rest of the Haldeman delegation froze for two hours each way in unheated trains.

Shortly after I returned to Peking from Canton, Sheldon "Shelly" Gold, an impresario from New York, arrived. He was interested in bringing Peking Opera to the States. As Jeff's client, Shelly took us to dinner where he talked about his world travels. I asked how his wife could bear for him to be so far away for so long. Didn't she miss him terribly?

Years later, when we were living in New York and Jeff traveled frequently to Asia, I thought about Shelly's wife in a different way. I wondered whether she had relished those blocks of time to herself as much as I did when Jeff traveled. For now, though, I was deep into a ménage à trois with Jeff and China. The three of us would even have a baby together.

MARRIED WITH KIDS

BEIJING BABY
1986

Jeff and I had been back in Manhattan long enough for me to have had three miscarriages and to have given birth in 1982 to our daughter, Eliza, who was now three. It was a typical day: telling Eliza my made up stories about a flying bunny named Brooklyn while pushing her stroller from our brownstone apartment to the 92nd Street Y Nursery School, stopping for groceries on the way home, and then practically turning right around to pick her up. On some mornings I fit in an appointment with one of the Park Avenue doctors who were trying to figure out why I was not holding my pregnancies. Jeff had been on a business trip to China for three weeks and was due home for the usual six weeks, in order to catch two ovulation cycles before heading back to the world's most populous country.

After school Eliza and I often stopped at a coffee shop and ate scrambled eggs while conversing as peers, though it was unclear whether she had risen to my level or whether I had descended to hers. During Jeff's absences, Eliza and I also went to fine restaurants, like one high above Central Park aptly named Nirvana, and enjoyed dinners that were more romantic than any Jeff and I went to when he was in town.

In fact, Jeff and I rarely went to restaurants. We preferred to be home with Eliza. On weekends, friends came over and we ordered take-out pasta, which we ate by moonlight on the small porch of our third-floor walk-up. Jeff and I also never took a vacation, just the two of us. The idea never even came up, because he endured excessive business travel and I never wanted to be apart from our daughter.

Despite all the joy Eliza provided, having only one child felt incomplete. Jeff and I were each one of three siblings, and we agreed that having three children seemed right for us, as though it were our genetic privilege. The likelihood of our producing more children came into question on that cloudless September afternoon when a hematologist phoned to say my blood tests revealed a borderline auto-immune condition that may have been preventing me from holding my pregnancies. I hung up wondering how I would reconfigure my lifelong assumption that as soon as I was ready to have children, pop, pop, pop, I would shoot them out.

As if on cue, Jeff called that evening from China to say he had to remain there for another month to work on a deal. He said I should take Eliza out of nursery school, which had begun only days earlier, and fly to Beijing (the new name for Peking) to be with him. Given that we had spent six weeks in China the previous spring, it felt soon for another lengthy stay.

I told him about the doctor's report, and then a thought occurred to me. "When we come, I'd like to adopt a baby," I said.

"Okay," he answered, as though I'd asked if we could get a new clock radio. How typical of Jeff to shrug and go along. My heart did a cartwheel.

China was not set up for foreign adoptions, but ever since we lived there for fifteen months in 1979, I periodically remarked to Jeff what a strong connection we both felt to the country and its people, and that someday we ought to adopt a Chinese child. I could barely sleep that night, making mental to-do lists and, alternately, gazing into the apple-seed eyes of my imaginary new baby. I was glad that on our last trip I had taken seat belts to install in the car we used there, so that would be one less thing to worry about. The following day I headed to Barnes & Noble to buy books about adoption, daring to believe we would be celebrating the new year with a new baby.

I realized, though, that the probability of the Chinese government blocking our efforts was high. Given my miscarriages, I had grown to anticipate disappointment. The frenzy that swirled about preparations for the trans-Pacific trip with a pre-schooler helped to tame some of my anxiety. As I piled clothes into an open suitcase on my bedroom floor and ran around buying snacks and toilet articles unavailable in Beijing, I wondered: *Will I love an adopted child as much as I love my biological child? Will my kid and I search for her birth parents?* And the "Que Sera, Sera" questions: *Will she be pretty? Will she be smart? (Will she be a girl?) Will we have rainbows day after day?*

Within a few days of Jeff's call, Eliza was sitting at my feet in the bulkhead of our United Airlines flight, painting her fingernails and her dress with fuchsia polish from her new manicure kit. I closed my eyes and reflected that had I carried my pregnancies to term, adopting a Chinese child probably would have remained lodged in my imagination, alongside my plan to study anthropology.

We landed in Tokyo where we transferred to a CAAC plane on which our tray tables would not stay in locked position. I had seen worse: standing room only on one flight I'd taken on the Chinese airline. Jeff greeted us in Beijing with the news that, while we were manicuring at 30,000 feet, his deal had fallen through. He was not suggesting that we return home, which was a good thing, since my deal—of tracking down a baby as well as permission from the Chinese government to adopt—was just beginning.

Eliza awoke early with an earache, which meant a trip to Capital Hospital. As if by design, the only other family in the foreigners' waiting area was a Caucasian couple with an Asian toddler, whose head had gotten bumped on a doorway while she was riding on her father's shoulders. I barely said hello before asking where their daughter was from. The mother told me they had adopted her in Hong Kong, which did nothing to advance my mission, though I stored this information in case mainland China didn't work out.

That afternoon, at the suggestion of our friend Xiao Hu, I went to the People's Court on Tiananmen Square. I told the man at the reception desk I would like to speak to someone about adopting a child. He said I would have to see the notary, and he led me around the corner to an uncluttered office with a high ceiling. The notary—who carried responsibilities different from those of notaries in the United States—looked about thirty years old and wore an oatmeal-colored cardigan with a hole at the elbow. He gestured for me to sit on a sofa that was covered with a thin, peach-colored terrycloth towel pulled tightly over the seat cushions and tucked in at the ends.

"What can I do for you?" he asked in heavily accented English.

"I'd like to adopt a Chinese child," I answered.

He inquired where I was from and whether I had any children. When I told him I had one daughter, he said nothing for what seemed like several minutes and then responded, "Since you already have one child, I am not sure this can be arranged."

Is he applying China's one-child policy to me? I wondered. I considered pointing out that if I were to adopt from Beijing, it would benefit the country, reducing its population by one. Instead, I said, "My husband and I can provide a wonderful home."

He looked pensive for a moment, then opened a drawer and took out paper and a pencil, which he set on a large, scratched, wooden table. "Please write why you want to adopt a Chinese child."

I wrote until my hand cramped about our happy home. Trying to come up with examples that would resonate, I included that we ate plenty of fresh fruits and vegetables with every meal. Sounding more like a politician than a parent, I pointed out the virtues of the health care and education we would provide. I also made sure to pepper this most important essay test of my life with words like "heartfelt" and "motherland," the kind of flowery language Chinese people used on the page. I read it over twice then handed it in, along with my fate, to this young fellow with the threadbare sleeve.

Back at the hotel, I phoned my friend Dr. Sun and told her I was in town. I had met Dr. Sun six years earlier in 1980 while giving a crash course on the logistics of life in the United States to a group of physicians who had anticipated traveling to the States to study. I always got together with them when I came to Beijing; this time, I hoped they might help me locate a baby. A few hours later, Dr. Sun called back to say she had arranged dinner with the group at the home of Dr. Chen.

At six p.m. I arrived with Chinese punctuality at the one-story courtyard home of Dr. Chen to find my nine former students—eight women and one man—already gathered. It reminded me of the class in which I had explained to them that in the U. S., it was okay for guests to arrive a bit late (which Chinese never did), but it was impolite to arrive early (which Chinese frequently did). Shortly after that lesson, I invited them to our hotel suite to learn how to eat spaghetti, peas, and chicken with forks and knives. They arrived en masse precisely fifteen minutes late. After the eating lesson I asked what they did on the one day a week they had off. "Laundry," said one. "I read medical journals," said another. Others said they did that too. They also unraveled their sweaters and re-knitted them to redistribute the worn parts.

Now, after the usual greetings and chitchat, I explained that I hoped to adopt a Chinese child, but first I needed to locate one. They all started clucking at once, like a bunch of yentas. Faster than it had taken for me to explain my mission, they came up with a plan. Dr. Yin said, "Here is what we can do. Many girls come to the hospital for abortions. When we see one who is pretty and intelligent, we must ask her to have the baby instead of aborting and we shall give the newborn to you." The others nodded agreement. Dr. Sun, an ob-gyn, said she would perform the delivery.

A friend later told me this scheme sounded outrageous.

Maybe I had spent too much time in China and was now thinking like a Chinese person, because I found the doctors' solution plausible. But if we pursued this idea, it would require waiting several months for the birth. What if the mother were to change her mind at the last minute? It became moot, as I had not yet realized that the easiest part of my endeavor would be turning up babies.

The following day, our friend Xiao Li came to see us. He was divorced and had a four-year-old daughter named Jing Jing. When I said I was looking into adoption, he offered us Jing Jing.

"Why would you adopt the child of a stranger," he asked, "when you can adopt one of someone you know?" Over the next few weeks, other Chinese friends and acquaintances asked us to adopt their children. Everyone wanted more for their kids than the dim prospects China offered. I cannot imagine that, under similar circumstances, I would have been able to make a sacrifice like that.

Our friend Xiao Hu knew an expectant couple; both were professors. They were considering getting divorced, and if so, they would welcome us to adopt the baby. The likelihood that this child would be intelligent was appealing, but there was too much uncertainty.

He knew another couple, who were paying severe tax penalties because they had three children. He said they would give up their six-month-old baby. How could they do that? It made me want to weep, but I considered it an option, until Xiao Hu added that they lived a thirteen-hour train ride away. That was too far to travel without knowing more. While waiting for a sure thing, I contemplated how dreadful Chinese life had been that so many parents were willing to part with their kids.

The optimist in me believed that the child meant for us was nearby. Most nights I stayed awake into the wee hours reading U.S. requirements for foreign adoptions and underlining segments in my adoption how-to books. One author cautioned that, unless you knew the family history, you were at risk of adopting a baby who was the result of incest.

"Yikes," I said to Jeff after reading it to him. He assured me that, in China, incest was virtually unheard of. The average Beijing resident lived jammed with relatives into playhouse-sized spaces; everyone knew everyone else's business; sex between family members was pretty unlikely. In addition, Chinese women seemed to have an innate sense of how to take care of themselves. I rarely saw them smoking or drinking.

During the days Eliza attended a nursery school where, alongside a roomful of Chinese children, she ate rice from a tin bowl and napped in a tiny bed. Jeff worked on deals that had not fallen through, ones he could just as well have worked on at home in New York. And I filled out U.S. forms that were required for adopting the child I had not yet located. I also contacted my Chinese friends from when we lived in Beijing six years earlier, to see if anyone could help us locate a baby.

One night at a business banquet, I sat next to a high-ranking official from the foreign ministry. I told him about my plight and he seemed to take an interest, so Jeff and he exchanged business cards. The following week we invited his family to dinner. Over a meal with him, his wife and their young daughter at a Western-style restaurant, we talked about life in the States. Jeff also told him about an American Express partnership he was working on and then described our efforts to adopt a Chinese baby.

It had been nearly a month since Eliza and I had arrived in Beijing, and Jeff said it was time to head back to the States. I told him that first I wanted to take the thirteen-hour train ride to meet Xiao Hu's friends with three children. That night, I received a phone call from Dr. Xiao, a gynecologist I had met the previous May when sex therapist Dr. Ruth Westheimer and her lawyer—a friend of ours—came to Beijing. Dr. Xiao was one of those I had called to say we were hoping to adopt.

"My niece works with a girl who is eight-and-a-half months pregnant," she said on the phone. "The girl thought she would be able to marry the child's father, but her *danwei* denied permission."

Nearly everything in China had to be approved by a person's *danwei* or work unit. I overcame my outrage at the government's control with the thrilling thought that this love child might just become our baby.

Jeff, ever the voice of what could go wrong, pointed out that if the newborn turned out to be a boy, the mother might decide to keep her son, despite the fact that a baby born out of wedlock would be a social outcast, denied even the right to attend school. I asked Dr. Xiao if she would arrange for the pregnant girl to see Dr. Sun for a check up.

Jeff and I sat on a wooden bench outside Dr. Sun's examining room at Beijing's Capital Hospital. Each time we heard the elevator door open down the hall, we inhaled, leaned forward in tandem, and turned our heads. When no pregnant teenager emerged, we leaned back, faced straight ahead again, and exhaled. Ordinarily we would be chatting about Eliza or Jeff's business; instead, I sat with my own thoughts and stared without focusing at the framed face of Chairman Mao on the cabbage green wall in front of me. In the dim yellow light, I was aware of doctors in white coats whizzing by and patients shuffling through my line of vision. Sounds of metal medical instruments clinked in the background.

For perhaps the sixth time, the pair of us angled forward. When a young girl—her belly protruding under a pilly, navy blue jogging suit—stepped out of the elevator, I inhaled so deeply that I gagged on the hospital's disinfectant fumes. The teenager clomped toward us, as though she were wearing over-sized clogs. Her hair hung straight down like a curtain over half her face. As she walked by, my eyes were drawn to her long tapered fingers; her hands looked like those of a pianist.

Just past us, she turned into the room to meet Dr. Sun. Fidgeting like the expectant parent I believed I was, I strained to hear their conversation, even though my Mandarin was inadequate.

I wished I could stroke her cheek and look into her face and have her look into mine. But Jeff said if she knew that an American couple was hoping to adopt her baby, she might demand a large sum of money. Rather, our investment amounted to the equivalent of twelve dollars for Dr. Sun to give the girl, so she could buy fruits and vegetables to eat during her final days of pregnancy. Of course we would also pay the hospital fees, which were only a few dollars. Our biggest outlay, sixty-six dollars, supplied chocolates for everyone who worked in the ob-gyn ward.

Rather than posing on this bench, I had come up with the idea that Jeff and I wear white coats and act as though we were visiting foreign doctors assisting Dr. Sun. There were a lot of restrictions in China, but at the same time, you could get away with things that would have been unheard of in the States. My craving to be in this pregnant girl's orbit trumped my judgment that such a charade would invade her privacy. Dr. Sun said it would be "simpler" if we pretended to be patients waiting in the hallway. This was the closest we would ever get to the pregnant young woman.

I could understand enough of the conversation to know that Dr. Sun was asking the questions I had given her from a list I had found in a book: Do you or your boyfriend wear glasses? Has either of you ever had acne? When did you get your first period?

Dr. Sun also asked the girl about her and her boyfriend's medical history: all four parents, but none of the eight grandparents, were alive. She said they all had died before the age of seventy. To a string of diseases and conditions—cancer, heart disease, stroke, kidney failure—my future child's birth mother responded, "*Mei you*," not have.

The young mother-to-be spoke in a high, sweet voice, the way actresses in early talkie films sounded. After the girl departed and the elevator doors closed behind her, Dr. Sun told us everything the girl had said, including that she liked to sing, read, and ice skate. *So do I*, I thought with glee, as if this childbearing factory worker and I would be able to curl up on a couch reading novels together or glide around the frozen moat of the Forbidden City arm in arm. Or, just maybe there was a baby inside of her who would someday read and skate with me.

Jeff, Eliza, and I returned to the States to complete paperwork, participate in a home study by a social worker, and await the birth of Eliza's sibling. Although I had never considered adopting a Caucasian baby, I wondered what it would be like to have a child of a different race.

The call came at 11:45 p.m. while I was in the bathtub and Jeff was asleep. I grabbed my robe without putting it on and ran to the phone. Jeff's secretary in Beijing said, "You have daughter!" "Oh my God! Oh my God!" I kept repeating while circling and circling the room. Imagine knowing your baby has just been born and it being too late to phone anyone to share the news. As for Jeff, I wanted him to be as excited as I was. He was so intent on getting his sleep that I was afraid if I woke him, he would say "hm, that's good" and then roll over and close his eyes. So with my heart thumping, I waited all the way till morning to share the news of our expanded family with Jeff and Eliza.

DEAR MOMS AND DADS

In 1979, China introduced its one-child policy to control population growth. The result was a decrease in births, but also an increase in the number of abandoned (and drowned) baby girls in this country that revered sons. By 1994, the Immigration and Naturalization Service would report the adoption of more than four thousand Chinese babies by U.S. citizens, but in the 1980s adoption was rare.

The Peking Hotel
Sat Nov 22, 1986

Dear Moms and Dads,

I'd like to write one of my marathon letters but between feeding Sabrina, playing with Lizie, napping, and arranging the baby's documents, there is time for little else. I must state the obvious, that adopting puts very little physical strain on the mom compared to giving birth. It helps that I have two nannies just about full time. The one who is forty-five calls the one who is fifty "Lao Tai Tai," which means Old Lady.

Sabrina is the model baby. She eats when she's supposed to, sleeps when she's supposed to and seems to enjoy being with us on the floor when we play games with Lizie, who wants to include her in everything, although every now and then Lizie gives the baby a good jab.

I've taken the girls out together twice—once to the park with Sabrina in her stroller and once for a walk near the hotel with the baby in the Snugli, which drew stares from every passerby.

So far it seems as though we are still a family of three, since Jeff has had to work almost around the clock. His business should lighten up by Thanksgiving. Some joint venture hotels are offering turkey dinners, so we'll go in the hope of having a satisfying meal.

Wednesday night we arrived in Beijing deep in the wee hours, and after dropping our bags at the hotel, we went to meet our darling new baby. The doctor led us through the hospital's dark empty halls to the nursery. They had wrapped Sabrina so tightly in a blanket that she looked like a lollipop or a drumstick. When a nurse picked her up, I snapped the baby's picture and she wailed. Clearly she was not as happy to see the three of us as we were to see her.

All along I had been sure I would want to take her back to the hotel the second we met her. But with her bawling and me collapsing from exhaustion after the long flight, I decided to wait.

The following afternoon, I went to the hospital and simply picked her up. Nothing to sign, they just handed her over. The head nurse permitted me to hire one of her staff for a few days at a cost of about two dollars a day. I learned the Chinese approach to caring for newborns. I must take the baby's temperature daily, she should drink water midway between feedings, and for a month she should not go anywhere and people should not come to see her.

So there we were: two nannies, one driver, the four of us, and twenty unpacked bags in a small, two-room suite. We stayed that way for a week until we moved to larger quarters where we are now quite comfortable.

I have spent much of my free time working on Sabrina's adoption papers and visa. On Friday we received her Chinese adoption certificate—it was effective exactly six weeks after we arrived in early October when I began my effort to adopt. The Chinese passport application went smoothly, other than trying to take photos of a two-week old sleeping baby where you want her eyes open and she shouldn't be crying. We expect to have the passport within a week.

That leaves only the U.S. visa to contend with—the biggest obstacle. A mid-January return to New York is likely, though I'm hoping for mid-December. In either case I'll be reluctant to give up the leisurely life here.

Eliza continues to live the life of Eloise, wreaking havoc in the Peking Hotel. Every day she visits her dad's office where no fewer than ten Chinese are ready to drop everything and play with her. A couple of times she has gone to a playgroup where one Malaysian women has fifteen children running around her living room. Either a nanny or I will stay the whole time because Eliza wants us to, and I feel a need to improve the adult-child ratio.

Every night we go to a different restaurant for a different bad meal. Sometimes we shop at the outdoor "free market," where clothing made for export is sold at a small fraction of the foreign retail price. Eliza has a few playmates her age, which is nice, but she misses her friends at home. One big event of the day is the six p.m. cartoon on TV.

The good thing about not sleeping much during our twelve days in N.Y. is that I had no jet lag when we returned here. Eliza says Sabrina is more fun than her doll, Folly, but not as much fun as a cat because a cat licks your toes.

Happy Thanksgiving—ours certainly is!

Love,
Susan

At the age of six weeks, Sabrina entered the United States. At five months, she became a U.S. citizen. Sabrina was a year old when Jeff attended a banquet in Beijing where he encountered the Chinese Foreign Ministry official whose family we had taken to dinner. The official told Jeff that the Chinese government had denied our request to adopt, but that he had intervened on our behalf. When Sabrina was sixteen months old, I gave birth to her sister, Emily, who was conceived as triplets, but when I had my first sonogram, there were three sacs but only one heartbeat.

FLYING THE COOP
1993

When Eliza was one year old, I was unwilling to make the trip from Manhattan to Staten Island for my cousin's wedding. I couldn't bear to be separated from my daughter by water.

Now, ten years and two kids later, I am about to take my first trip without my girls. I start worrying six weeks beforehand, the day I sign up for a writing seminar in Key West. What if they're riding on the Expressway and a driver sneezes? You can't keep your eyes open when you sneeze. What if someone who works the night shift dozes off at the wheel?

Can I trust that someone will hold Sabrina's and Emily's hands while walking to school? Without watchful eyes on her, Sabrina can wind up in the middle of the road.

Weeks pass and my anxiety shifts. What if something happens to me? Is it fair to take the chance that the plane will crash, leaving my daughters motherless? I wish I could grasp what keeps planes aloft as clearly as I understand gravity.

Now that I have carried the seminar plans this far, I can't live with myself if I am such a wimp that I don't go. Not an hour passes that I don't worry. Finally I take the leap and make air reservations.

Thirty minutes after I pay for a seat on the commuter flight from Miami to Key West, I hear on the news that an identical plane has crashed in the Midwest. I book my room at a B & B, which I'll cancel when I change my mind about going.

On the morning I am to leave, the alarm beeps at four-thirty, awakening me from a dream where someone is stealing my wallet. I wish I could go back to the mugging. A while later I am on the plane with seat belt fastened, and a funny thing happens. All tension flows from my body. I am help-lessly in the hands of fate. As with roller coasters, once the bar snaps shut, you are on your way, and there is no revers-ing the bad decision you made to go in the first place.

I worry that phone calls with the kids will be frustrating and unsatisfying, but I am tempted to pick up the Airfone that is glaring from the seatback in front of me. I postpone until evening the urge to call home. Instead I pull out the envelope of photos I hastily prepared last night. I wonder why I chose pictures from Halloween. Two sad clowns and a hippie.

Later, when I phone home, Jeff picks up. "They're all sick," he says. "And sluggish."

This is good news. Staying home from school means they won't be crossing streets. "I have the French bread pizza in the oven," he tells me. I had left twenty heat-and-serve meals in the freezer.

These first twelve hours have yielded nothing worse than

a rash all over Emily's body, a fever for Eliza, and a headache for Sabrina, who gets a migraine if you ask her to tie her shoes. It's a successful start.

Another funny thing happens. I don't miss them. During my lunch break the following day, I lie on the beach eating a banana and reading a book, feeling wild and frivolous.

Not wanting the children to think I have forgotten them, I again phone home before dinner. They have rented three videos and everyone is feeling better. When I am home, there is limited TV and lots of vegetables. I begin to suspect they don't miss me either. Jeff sounds particularly merry.

On the day of my departure for home, the airline calls to say my flight has been cancelled. Due to a snowstorm up north, they are consolidating the schedule. They book me on a later flight, which means the children will be asleep when I get home.

I get religious when I fly. The nineteen-seater from Key West lands safely at Miami International; in appreciation I promise God I'll volunteer at a homeless shelter. I reflect on all the anxiety I'd had about the little plane I just took, yet I am now relatively sanguine about taking this 757. If defying gravity is what scares me, shouldn't huge jets be *more* worrisome?

On my endless walk through the terminal's corridors, I pass several large TV screens where clusters of travelers are watching CNN. A major earthquake has devastated Los Angeles. I make a pact with myself never, ever to go to L.A.

I reach the gate, where an earlier flight is about to board. Standby passengers hoping for seats are hanging on the desk, trying to extract information from agents who are smiling through clenched teeth.

One of these planes may crash. I don't know which one.

So I am not going to knock myself out to get on the earlier flight, and then learn I made a bad choice. I'll leave it to chance. Plus, with a reservation on a plane leaving later, that is two more hours I'll have to myself.

DISCONNECTED
1993

The person I see most often these days is the fruit man. Even when I do not need anything, I bike the mile into town and buy oranges at his stand behind the local hardware store, just so I can hear him ask, "How're ya doin' today?"

By answering, "Fine," I reassure myself that it's so.

"Take this rhubarb muffin to Eliza from me," George says one morning. "Tell her to play at a lower altitude next time." My fruit man knows my daughter fell out of a tree last week; my friends do not.

I wish that this, my one steady relationship aside from my family, were based on more than dietary fiber. But social bonding requires time, the precious spare moments I reserve for myself.

Still, how long can I continue on this dubious path of being my own best friend before I reach a point where I have no one to call in a crisis? I like to think old friends will be there—when the time comes—to help me face things like living with three adolescent daughters and burying my dog, if I had a dog. I'll want to be there when their dogs die too.

Jeff and I are a good match. He travels a lot and I'm a solitudinarian. When he is away, I stay up late, wallowing in my quiet quarters; the only socks on the bedroom floor are mine. Why don't I use his business trips as an opportunity to keep up with friends? Is it possible that insufficient time is not the real culprit?

Without an everyday confidante, there was no one to call while anticipating my solo trip to Key West. I had to brood alone about leaving my kids motherless in the event of an air tragedy. (Jeff would have none of it.) The vision of my daughters in black velvet hair bows tossing roses on my casket haunted me every night when I closed my eyes. It was not the kind of thing I could whine about to a pal I hadn't spoken to since Flag Day.

Otherwise, this is a fine relationship I have with myself. When I go to movies, for example, I take pleasure in being alone, although sometimes I go with Jeff out of nuptial responsibility. Why are films I see myself always better? Because there is no one next to me squirming and looking at his watch, that's why.

On the other hand, I don't mind suspending disbelief at a PG film with a kid on each side and one on my lap and enough popcorn to last a double feature. At the sappy parts, I shed tears I would be embarrassed to have anyone over twelve witness.

So, you see, I have pushed everything aside, the way you make room for coats in the hall closet when company's coming. I have made good use of that space, filling it with my kids, my husband, and my precious solitude. All that's missing is the company.

My seclusive behavior may explain why I did not find out

my best friend was mugged until five days later. Years ago, I would have known immediately; we talked every time either of us sat down to breast-feed. My other best friend lives three hundred miles away. We talk quarterly.

As my firstborn became more independent, so did I. No longer was the telephone cord my lifeline. Now, years later, I lament that the messages on my answering machine tend to be from an appliance store selling service contracts and the pediodontist saying the kids are due for checkups. I am glad, at least, that I do not have to spend time calling anyone back.

It wasn't always this way. Like the heroine in a novel I once read, I have a box of memories. It safeguards such relics as the clay penis Luke made in art class and the diary in which I listed the kids I talked to each day. Back then, I never said good-bye to my girlfriends. Instead I'd say, "Call me." Then when they called and we finished talking, I would say, "I'll call you later."

When did things change? The first time I lived alone, my neighbor, seeing my lamp go on, would phone every evening as soon as I walked in the door. It was then I discovered that soaking in a warm tub gave me more pleasure than exchanging details of a day that bore an unsettling resemblance to the one before. Finally, I gently asked her not to call every time the window lit up. She understood, yet was available twenty-four hours a day for a chat and a cup of coffee, which gave me both the space and intimacy I desired.

I have moved nine times and lived in three different countries since then. In each new place it gets harder to know the neighbors. There are days I want to call "Hiya!" over the back fence to someone who, like me, has kids young enough to be her grandchildren. Then hash out why I'm sometimes frazzled, scrambling to find time to recline with a book and believing the day is a failure if I don't. Jeff will not give the subject thirty seconds. For this I need an everyday friend. Ethel Mertz. A soul mate who drops in for coffee but doesn't stay longer than the time it takes to go from one commercial to the next.

It could be all the relocating that has unglued me from my day-to-day contacts. Ironically, moving from Manhattan to nearby Long Island made me feel more detached than when I moved from Manhattan to Hong Kong.

Living abroad, I had an excuse not to phone. Instead, I wrote letters that were so long I included a table of contents. I recorded details about the Filipina beauty contest I was asked to judge and about the marines from Speedwell, Virginia (pop. 635) we invited for Thanksgiving dinner. Simply writing about my problems—and the presumption that someone was listening—helped me cope. It was easy to make thirty photocopies and mail them. Instant connection. Returning to my roots was harder. I felt more in touch through those chronicles than I had when living only a few blocks from someone. In the States I have less control; relationships have to be two-way.

Sometimes I envy my cousin Karen. She spends so much time on the phone that she knows five married women who are having affairs. I don't know a single one. People used to confide in me when I kept in touch. These days, I talk on the phone only while preparing dinner. It is hard to express empathy for someone's sex life while skinning the broccoli stems and trying to keep my kids from massacring one another during the pre-meal frenzy. For me, though, talking on the telephone and not doing something else at the same time is as unlikely as sitting on a porch rocker without a kid on my lap.

Karen turned fifty this year. She threw herself a birthday

bash where she recited her history with each person there. The more she spoke, the gloomier I felt. I hit bottom at the part where she and Maggie laughed their way across Europe the summer after their junior year. (Why is someone else's connectedness so unsettling? Do I really want what Karen has, or am I just being competitive?)

I went to Europe that summer too. It turned out to be wholly satisfying to journey solo, indulging my own whims and taking meals in the company of a good book I could close at will. Meeting people was also easier when I was alone. Available. There is something about the seduction of a new relationship.

At times, though, the whole world seemed to be connected, except for me. One morning I woke up in my *pensione* room on the Costa Brava and heard someone outside say, "There are people on the moon." With no one to turn to, I thought, *Wow, our first astronauts have landed on the moon and they found people living up there!*

If the social opportunities provided by trips to the fruit man and visits from the handyman are not enough to satisfy me, then what's to stop me from seeing one friend each week? But who? Where do I start? Do I really want to be involved in another person's daily life?

After Karen's birthday, I decided that once a year I would visit friends in D.C. where I lived for more than a decade. Those were my single years, when I had a dozen intimates and spent most of my spare time sitting over quiche and onion soup with one or another of them, talking about boys. The subject never wore thin. I wonder if analyzing the safety features of Volvos or the merits of tracking in the schools, while picking at a tri-color salad and a sliver of eight-grain bread, could ever be as electrifying.

Pursuing short cuts to intimacy, I have become skilled in the art of the four-minute tête-à-tête. Last week I picked up seven-year-old Sabrina at her friend Kate's house and had the longest chat with a female over twelve that I'd had in a month. While my daughter tied her shoes, I told Kate's mom, Judy, about my irregular pap smear and how it drives me crazy when Jeff works at home. These conversation bites would satisfy me if I had one every day. Or would they?

The only time Judy and I spend together is when we exchange kids, yet she knows more about what is going on in my world than do lifelong friends whose children live too far to play with mine. She once confided that she is out of touch too. I felt an instant bond and enormous relief not to be alone in my solitude. Then I remembered that her grade school chum is her neighbor. When you live close enough to smell the coffee of someone with whom you share a past, you are not disconnected.

It troubles me that after a gunman opened fire on a train near my home, the only one who phoned to see if I was okay was my mom. I talked to her about my isolation and about how I get breathless when I think about time running out. "You work too hard," she said. I understand why she sees it that way. When she was my age, she did not stay home and write about her life; she went to charity lunches. Now, in Florida, she goes to early-bird dinners with different friends every night and participates in organized activities, like rap sessions for seniors.

My mother used to say, "If books are your friends, you'll never be lonely." Books are indeed my friends, but they don't leave messages on my answering machine.

NIGHT OWL
1993

The moment I cross the sleeping car's threshold, my universe contracts to the size of the Magnavox console TV we got when I was six. Styrofoam has not been invented and distant lovers communicate with fountain pen on scented pages. Yet the present has a way of intruding. Instead of a war hero blowing farewell kisses to my fluttering hanky, Nancy, the porter, shoos me inside the slumber coach so she can secure it against muggers.

Nine-thirty p.m. I slide shut the heavy metal door of my compartment and then sink into the mattress, encased by a picture window on one side, a mirrored panel on the other. A hinge supports the foot of my bed; the head rests on a small toilet. This lone sleeping car will remain motionless in a remote corner of New York's Penn Station until three-thirty, when it will hook up with the Night Owl from Boston, ballooning the usual four-hour ride to Washington into an overnight adventure. I like being smack up against the glass. In the morning, even if I face the other way, I can spy in backyards through the reflection in the mirror. It reminds me that I am not the only one with broken clay pots outside the kitchen door.

Satisfied that I tucked in my kids at home and will get a full night of sleep, yet still be on time for my rendezvous with college classmates in D.C., I turn out the lights, except for the blue one above my pillow, and then mentally transform myself into Claudette Colbert. I imagine myself heading to Florida, as she did in the 1942 comedy *The Palm Beach Story*. I fancy myself wearing striped men's pajamas on a diesel train. Rudy Vallee is down the hall.

Once, before a trip on the Broadway Limited, I searched men's shops for the perfect pair of oversized pajamas. What is this nostalgic pull, this identity with the past, as though setting foot in a Pullman endows me with a 1940's soul and gleaming red toenails that peek out of wedge-heeled shoes? The truth is I eschew ruby nail polish and open-toe wedgies. These ornaments of womanhood make me feel too much like my mother.

Sometimes my reverie links me to a different past: sitting ramrod straight in the parlor car, I am on my way to Grandma's, the tips of my patent leather skimmers grazing the floor. (Actually, my grandparents lived two blocks from school. Every day at three I tore over to their house—in my Buster Browns—where they plied me with Coca-Cola and sour pickles.)

Whether my fantasy has me off to Palm Beach in a screwball comedy without a buck in my pocket or on a journey to a farmhouse filled with baking smells, I feel protected. Embraced by a prior era, I long for the days when mothers were neither bank managers nor porters, but warm bodies in fruited aprons who read picture books to their kids in which locomotives were underdogs who triumphed.

I put my daydreams on pause to reach down for my nightshirt. Under the bed, amid dust balls, I spy a small cardboard tent. Printed above an adhesive strip are the words Trapper Mouse Pro. While I am charmed by rodents, the Hunca Munca variety who wear pinafores and tidy up doll houses, I hope to be spared from sharing my cabin with one.

I raise the shade to peer out while conducting my periodontal regimen. A woman wearing tan pumps is standing near my window. Although I am at eye level with the hem of her brown tweed skirt, I lean back, so she won't see me floss. Would my gums flare up if I skipped flossing just this once? I choose not to risk it. The minutiae that clutter my daily life have accompanied me here as surely as have my intestines.

Ten forty-five p.m. Several stories below Thirty-Third Street and Eighth Avenue (you could have a clandestine affair here and no one but Porter Nancy would suspect), I imagine what's going on overhead. A panhandler soliciting dollars for a latte? A stickup in a shop that sells bogus I.D.?

Or worse. I recall the words of the Amtrak agent when I arrived early.

"You're entitled to wait in the Metropolitan Lounge."

"I didn't realize Penn Station had a lounge," I replied.

"Well, it was closed for a time. We had a violent incident."

"Violent?"

"Yeah. A guy, well, killed a woman there. You know how it goes sometimes." I don't, but I convince myself I am secure, entombed by the carpeted walls of my couchette. Relishing

137

my solitude, I slip between the threadbare sheets. After reading three paragraphs, I nod off, grateful to have had the opportunity to read at all without interruption by three daughters who seem drawn to me whenever I recline.

I am bumped awake when they harness us to the rest of the train. As long as I'm up, I'll pee. I always have to go when I know how inaccessible the toilet is. Raising the bed with my left hand, I use my right to lift the toilet cover. The left hand remains extended to prevent the bed from squashing me. I reverse the procedure then crawl back under the covers.

The side-to-side rocking lulls like a colossal iron cradle. Suddenly a rattle jolts me out of my alpha stage. Like a madwoman I dart around, wedging folded rectangles of toilet paper between any two things that move. Then I give up and stop noticing, until a squeak catches my attention. The Trapper! I hang upside down to check. Thank God it's empty. I wonder how Nancy feels about mice.

Four-forty a.m. As we roll toward Trenton I sandwich my head in a fold of the pillow, trying to remember what is so seductive about spending the night on a train. Is it simply a unique chance to read three paragraphs in seclusion, no one grousing that I blow my nose too loud while he is trying to sleep? When boarding after a lengthy interlude, I tingle as though I have been reunited with a lover and am smelling his neck for the first time in ages.

Outside, the silhouetted landscape refuses to be transfixed by my gaze. Black sky, like snow, is a great equalizer; every row house, every Main Street shows no blemish. If I squint, a power plant, with its thousands of tiny lights, resembles a carnival. The world is in disguise, safe, incognito, if only for one night. While inside, I have my own masquerade.

In August, 1994, after nearly ten years of service, Amtrak discontinued the Executive Sleeper, the overnight train between New York and Washington.

Havin' a Snow Ball
and Lessons Learned
1996

Day one. It is not easy to remain asleep knowing that overnight huge frosty marshmallows have formed on our azaleas during the first big snow since our move last summer from New York to D.C. I spring out of bed eager for fun in the snow with my three daughters.

Though I cannot account for the time, an hour passes. I am deep in the hall closet, sweating and searching for mittens; coats draped over my polar-fleeced buttocks muffle the whining of Sabrina and Emily, who are now nine and seven.

"Where's my other leg warmer?"

"I can't get these pants over my boots."

Jeff lumbers downstairs. I transfer pandemonium management to him and exit through the kitchen door.

"You're stepping on my toboggan run!" Eliza shrieks. The alternative is a drift as high as my hip. I begin to wade solo up the street, my Flexible Flyer in tow. A family of five pauses to say hi. Envious, I wonder how they managed to leave their house as a unit.

Emily bounces across our yard to catch up with me. We fold ourselves onto the Flyer but must paddle in order to blaze a trail. I never imagined such a thing as too much snow (lesson 1).

Sabrina waddles out to join us. Jeff has bundled her in four layers and—oh no—my new chenille scarf. The girls coast smoothly on my sled, while I twirl behind in slow motion on their turquoise saucer. On the next run, hoping for a greater thrill, I pile on with them.

My added weight imbeds the runners into the soft snow. Sledding with the kids is better in concept than in reality (lesson 2).

We wave to the family unit who are now on their way home. It cheers me that our outing is lasting longer than theirs. A cross-country skier whoops as she schusses past. Skiing is what I want to be doing, yet I could never enjoy it if I did not first sled with the kids; it is not guilt that drives me, but an obsession that I might miss a moment of their childhood fun. (There is a lesson here, but I have not figured out what it is.)

Day two. Unlike yesterday, I arise with trepidation. The storm has been raging throughout the night; you can no longer see that we have azaleas.

I am not ready to take on the kids. Where can I hide? The empty bathtub! I pad it with towels and settle in with my journal while Jeff sleeps. Stretched out in the tub, I experience the most peace I have found since the storm began (lesson 3).

Jeff awakens and announces his plan to take a train to New York for his meeting tomorrow. Is it annoyance or envy that shoots through me? Given the weather, Broadway theaters will be half-empty; I imagine him getting an orchestra seat. He will feast on *zuppa di pesce* at Divino, our favorite Italian restaurant. As for me, I shall be grateful for one less set of boots and mufflers in the front hall.

After promises to return from my solo outing with cocoa and Jell-O, I get out of the house in record time. It pays to bribe (lesson 4).

I step into my cross-country skis, and travel two miles to the supermarket. In poultry, I stuff a package of chicken breasts into my pocket to see if it will fit for the ski ride home. A woman fondling turkey parts gives me a look.

I pay, and with my jacket evenly weighted, I cruise to Starbucks where my friend Alan is standing at the end of a long line. We reminisce about the blizzard of '78—the desperate trek to get a coffee chip cone at Hagen Dazs. Now, it's a cafe mocha at Starbucks. "How far we have not come," he says. The whole idea makes me feel old and young at the same time.

Day three. I phone roofers about the drips that began trickling from my bedroom ceiling at the exact moment Jeff left for New York. Emily interrupts my third conversation with an answering machine. She complains that Sabrina won't stop singing "This is the song that never ends. Yes, it goes on and on my friend . . . *(repeat forever)*"

Emily gets the idea to retaliate with "I know a song that gets on everybody's nerves, everybody's nerves, everybody's nerves, and this is how it goes . . . *(repeat forever)*"

Four hours later I am still in my nightgown. Eliza, the only one I wanted here so she could baby-sit while I ski, has gone sledding with a neighborhood friend. Emily is nagging, "There's nothing to do." I tell her to go eat the gingerbread house Sabrina made last month.

The sky is the color of soot and falling flakes are teeny and dense. Lighten up, I tell myself, and relish this phenomenon of nature (lesson 5). What I cannot relish is watching nine hours of weather reports the way Jeff did on Sunday, flipping channels to find another weatherman every time a report ended.

Day four. Sabrina and Emily are playing tug-of-war with my chenille scarf, which I hope will buy me enough time to write a few tips for my article about coping with snow days. My real problem is that I want to make a snowman and watch movies and bake cookies and can't seem to settle down with any one of these without feeling tormented that I'm missing out on the others.

My friend Jackie calls and I whine to her about having too many options. "Don't try to do everything," she says. "Just do one really great thing each day (lesson 6)." Jackie is a low-metabolism type who considers the day a triumph if she gets to take a bath instead of a shower. I wonder whether people with fewer expectations are happier. I type Jackie's advice onto my tips list, knowing I'll never follow it.

The children are delighted by the all-white dinner—mashed potatoes, noodles, and rice pudding—I bring home from the nearby gourmet market. Before falling asleep, I vow that tomorrow I shall do not one great thing, but six: sled, ski, light a fire, watch TV with the kids, drink cocoa, and munch popcorn. With my daughters silenced by slumber, I can afford to be optimistic.

Day five. Last night's vow gets broken early on. No one wants to sled with me. Even Emily has had it with fun in the snow. I, myself, admit to being a trifle bored with skiing; it is far more tantalizing when not quite so available (lesson 7).

The family TV concept has deteriorated into them against me: they want *Animaniacs*, while I was hoping for *Tammy and the Bachelor*. I cannot get the flue open and we have run out of Swiss Miss and microwave popcorn. We settle for toasting marshmallows over a candle, cleaning up the mess it causes, and then watching Oprah while gorging on saltines.

During a commercial Jeff returns from New York, and before even kicking off his boots, he clicks to the Weather Channel.

Day six. In keeping with the urge to indulge that the snow has aroused in me, I call my friend Pam and sit still for an entire hour while we speak. I never just talk on the phone. I double task with knee bends or flossing, two teeth at a time. Giving my full attention to the conversation with Pam is like eating an entire fudge pie with nothing to dilute the richness (lesson 8).

I fall asleep worrying that our supplies are dwindling. I consider door-to-door bartering: a can of SpaghettiOs for a roll of Charmin (lesson 9).

Day seven. I am dismayed that I cannot account for my time this past week. On my to-do list I write "make activity list" so I'll be prepared for the next storm (lesson 10).

Outside I encounter an unanticipated sight: snow plows. Three of them. My throat constricts at the thought of driving to get groceries. I have grown fond of this life in which I ski to the market to stock the fridge. It is only minor solace that the plow in front of my house is skidding. How can a snow plow get stuck in the snow?

Pale yellow winter sky fades into steely blue. The helpless plows look like buffalo flailing on a frozen landscape. The girls and I prepare sandwiches and a thermos of hot coffee for the drivers, who persist in trying to make it up our block. One plow breaks loose and slams into a fire hydrant from which a rapid river erupts. The crew promises to return in the morning. Should we serve waffles or pancakes?

Now we have an unplowed street and no plumbing. That suits me, for it is too soon for navigable roads to put the kibosh on this life-sustaining routine that was so hard to establish but will be so hard to give up.

I shiver at the thought of returning to goals that require more thinking than how much salt to sprinkle on the path in case the mailman ever shows up again.

"I May Have Ruined
The Marriage, But You're
Ruining The Divorce"
1996 - 1997

Jeff gave me an obligatory peck on the cheek, turned and
blew extra kisses to the girls, and then dashed to the
Wilmington rail platform to catch his train back to New York.
In our idling station wagon, Emily and Sabrina, ages eight and
nine, munched on rice cakes, crumbs falling all over the back
seat. Thirteen-year-old Eliza was at sleep-away camp. As the
locomotive rolled out of the station, I slid over to the driver's
seat and shifted out of park.

The four of us had spent the weekend visiting friends at their
beach house, and now the two girls and I were heading home
to D.C. Jeff had a place in Manhattan because he worked there
a few days a week. I liked this part-time-husband arrangement:
having the kids to myself, making French toast for dinner, eating dinner in the bathtub if we felt like it. When Jeff first told me
about the New York apartment, he explained that it belonged to
a fellow who had moved temporarily to Hong Kong. That's why

there was no phone number. The phone, Jeff said, rang directly into an answering machine so the owner could pick up his messages. Jeff was reachable on his cell phone.

I wanted to know how to reach him in an emergency in case his cell phone wasn't on. So he gave me the address, which I wrote on a green Post-it that I taped to the fridge to make sure it wouldn't fall off.

As I was pulling out of the railway station's parking lot, I froze. I realized that Jeff had been in such a hurry that he had left his keys dangling from the ignition. All I could think was, *If I call him later and he's in the apartment, that will mean he got in because he has a girlfriend.*

Given the amount Jeff traveled, I had decided early in our marriage that there was no use worrying whether he was fooling around. The jealousy would have made me crazy. Plus, this was a guy who paid his taxes. I trusted him.

But his back and forth to New York seemed different. Jeff grumbled a lot about our move to Washington, which I had orchestrated. Even before we relocated, he had sometimes acted so remote that it worried me. Was this to be our relationship into our mom-mom and pop-pop stage and beyond?

After a year in D.C., I suggested we consult a couples' therapist. Our first appointment with Dr. Weiss was striking only because she looked so much like our friend Laurie that it felt like she *was* Laurie. For our second session, Jeff had to go to a meeting in New York at the last minute, so rather than cancel I went alone.

Toward the end of the visit, Dr. Weiss asked, "Have you ever wondered whether Jeff is living the bachelor life in New York?" No I hadn't, until you asked.

That was the last time I saw Dr. Weiss, but her words rearranged my brain and ultimately my life. Questions started popping into my head. "How do your sheets get washed?" I asked my husband that evening.

"I take them down the block to the Chinese laundry," he answered without hesitation.

During the three-hour drive home from Wilmington, I searched my mind for scenarios of how Jeff would manage without his keys. All I came up with was a buxom, long-haired blonde—wearing scant, black lace panties and bra—opening the door for him. Clues from the past wove figure eights through my thoughts.

There was the previous Thanksgiving when we took our daughters to New York for the holiday. I had suggested we go to see his apartment. "Nah," he said. "There's nothing to see."

I kept pressing and he kept saying nah until finally—ever the risk-taker—he said okay. Was this really a risk-taking streak or was he just being Jeff, who in his personal life preferred to agree rather than argue? If he had something to hide, what was his plan B? I helped him out, because when he finally said we could go, I decided it would be a waste of time. Or, was I afraid of what clues I would find there?

In my haze I made it home from Wilmington through a steady glare of oncoming headlights. Hurriedly, I tucked in my girls—quick kisses, no bedtime story—so I could call Jeff.

Trying to control my breathing, which had been off and on either too deep or too shallow, I dialed his number.

He answered his cell phone in his usual cheery tone.

"You forgot your keys," I said. "How'd you get into your apartment?"

"I keep a spare set in my briefcase," he answered breezily. He always had an answer. And that was that, until later in the summer.

While Eliza was still at camp, we rented a cottage on Long Island in the village of Amagansett. On a sunny Wednesday, Sabrina, Emily, Jeff, and I enjoyed a lazy afternoon on the beach, reading, playing ball, and swimming. We returned to our place for an early barbecue, during which Jeff—as he often did—initiated a game of "Name that Tune" by humming the first two notes of "Sixteen Tons." Before nightfall, I drove him to the train station. He had an eight o'clock meeting in the city the following morning.

An hour or so later, the telephone rang. It was Jeff. He had borrowed someone's cell phone to let me know he had lost his own phone.

A few hours after that, Jeff's friend and business associate Tony called from China. I told Tony that Jeff had gone to New York and had lost his cell phone. And then it occurred to me to see whether Tony could provide a link to the mystery of Jeff's apartment.

"You have his number in the city, don't you?" I asked. I stopped breathing.

He replied, "You mean . . . " and recited the phone number. It felt like Tony had just hauled a dodge ball into my gut, yet I managed to commit the number to memory.

The second we hung up I dialed. I was counting on Jeff to once again provide a glib explanation.

"How come you answered this phone?" I asked when Jeff picked up.

"How come I answered?" he said, which I later recognized as a way to buy a few seconds to come up with a plausible response. He rambled about one phone being forwarded to another and something about the answering machine. It was becoming harder for me to suspend disbelief.

The following morning I awoke to an overcast sky, so the girls and I went to paint pottery. I promised we would go out afterward to a real nice lunch, an activity that no doubt pleased me more than it did them. At the pottery place, I chose a napkin holder to work on. I painted a family of five seated around a dinner table on one side. On the other side, with no awareness of irony, I painted a glass of milk that had tipped over and the words, *Don't cry over spilt milk.*

The moment I finished, like a thunderclap, the whole episode with Tony from the night before came back to me. I was exploding to call the number that obviously rang in Jeff's apartment. Spotting a pay phone outside, I said, "I'll be right back, girls."

With trembling fingers, I dialed. I had no plan for what I'd do if someone actually answered, so I gasped when I heard a woman say, "Hello." Not wanting to arouse suspicion by hanging up, I asked, "Is Carol there?" The absurdity of my worrying about arousing suspicion, as though I were the one violating a vow, escaped me.

"There is no Carol here," she said in a Chinese accent. I hung up with my head pulsating, my mind concocting explanations. It's possible she's a housekeeper I thought. But I knew it was far more likely she was Jeff's girlfriend. I felt myself spiraling around Jeff as I moved in for the kill. An orgasmic urge came over me to get back to our cottage so I could start calling friends. I needed help sorting this out.

"Change of plans," I told the girls. "C'mon, hurry up, we're gonna grab some pizza then go back and watch TV." This TV suggestion was way out of character for me but, hey, the kids were not about to question it.

I ordered nothing, just sat there in the pizza place, jiggling my feet while the girls ate with tiny bites. After lunch, we returned to our cottage where I deposited Sabrina and Emily in front of the television. I then took the cordless phone outside and sat with my feet up on a chair by the table at which the night before we'd eaten hamburgers and sung oldies. The sky was still overcast.

I dialed Robert, an old friend who had divorced his wife a long time ago and was now remarried. "Do whatever you can to stay married," he said. "Divorce is awful when you have kids. I say that even though I've been happily remarried for ten years."

Next I called Sheila, a psychotherapist I had seen a few times. She said if we ended up getting divorced, the best interests of the children should drive all subsequent decisions. She had once told me there were different kinds of marriages and had described Jeff's and mine as a "business marriage."

Jeff was a skillful lover and our sexual relationship was satisfactory, if not frequent. I worried more about whether we were having as much sex as other couples than I did about actually having more sex. We each went about our own lives while sharing responsibilities and devotion to the family.

In other words, there was not an abundance of passion, but our arrangement afforded us a happy family life and the independence we both craved.

I did not question the role I played—as a semi-detached, child-absorbed spouse—in his straying (if indeed he had strayed), though perhaps I should have, not that it would have in any way excused his behavior. Did I even love him? Did he love me?

It was hard to say how much my own feelings of distance resulted from the vibe I got from him. For instance, the day I returned from a week at a writing workshop in Vermont, he was on the soccer field watching the kids play. I headed directly there and when I approached him, he continued watching and stuck out his face for me to kiss his cheek.

I recalled the period when Jeff and I were still single and enjoying daily robust sex. He once said married people ought to be able to have sex with other partners. I shrugged off his comment, believing he was kidding. Now I wondered.

Naturally, there were men who had attracted me after Jeff and I wed. When we lived on Long Island, there was the Croatian with strong, hairless forearms who lived across the street and spoke barely any English, whom I could watch sawing in his driveway from my desk at a second story window, while Jeff was negotiating deals with Asian businessmen and my children were learning long division. If, on a drizzly afternoon, he had glanced up and beckoned, would I have resisted? But no one made advances. Since I had attracted guys before Jeff, I reasoned that my body gave off a "married" chemical that kept men away. Of all the debris swirling around my mind that bleak night in Amagansett, one fleeting thought titillated me: if we were to divorce, I would again get a shot at romantic love.

Another memory surfaced. On our three-hour drive to Long Island a few days earlier, while the kids dozed in the back seat, something about AIDS came on the radio and I said to Jeff, "I can't understand how anyone could cheat these days, with the risk of giving their spouse HIV." He nodded and uttered, "Mm-hmm."

The sky was growing dark now and the girls had not stirred from their post at the TV. After talking to a half dozen friends, a plan gelled in my mind. I needed confirmation that I was not making false assumptions about Jeff having another woman.

Afraid I'd lose my courage, I quickly dialed the number from Tony. My stomach flip-flopped when the woman answered. "May I please speak to Jeff?" I asked, raising my voice a few notes in case she recognized it from my earlier call.

"There is no Jeff here," she said.

"Oh," I answered. "This is George Goodman's secretary. Jeff gave George this number. George needs to speak to him as soon as possible." Like Tony, George was a good friend and business associate. I figured she would know his name.

"Jeff is not here now. I do not know where he is." Her response confirmed my suspicions.

Feeling strangled by a twisted cord of both belief and disbelief, I whispered, "Thank you." And I hung up.

At some point, I must have offered the children dinner and tucked them in with hugs, but all I remember is sitting outside, stunned under the black sky, riveted to that chair. At one point the phone rang and I startled. It was Jeff calling to say he would be back around midnight.

A little before twelve I went inside and waited, my whole body quaking. Soon Jeff walked through the door, unaware that his life was about to change forever. In a soft, innocent tone I asked, "So tell me again why you answered the phone last night? I thought you never used that number."

Making a back and forth pouring motion with his hands, he started explaining again how one phone rings into another. I interrupted him with carefully chosen words. "Okay, enough. I called tonight and had a conversation with your friend. I know what you've been up to, so why don't you tell me the whole story."

His face turned the color of cardboard. His lips pursed

and his cheeks puffed out as though filled with vomit. He then sat down. I asked how they met, when they met, where they met. If for no other reason than he didn't know how much I knew, I believe he answered my questions truthfully.

Then a weird thing happened. All of a sudden I felt myself attracted to him, the way you feel about a new lover. Unfortunately, though, this was too serious to be a make-up sex opportunity. I told Jeff to sleep on the sofa. It was like I was now living inside a cliché; the next steps were HIV tests and therapy.

The following morning I woke up foggy from a splintered sleep, still in shock. What are you supposed to do when you are on a beach vacation with your kids, and your husband has just bloodied you with betrayal? You make pancakes and pack up turkey sandwiches for lunch.

Jeff and I slouched in our beach chairs, alternating between silences and my questions to which he gave no answers. "How could you do this?" "Why did you do this?"

In a compartment of my purse, along with my driver's license and coffee discount cards, I had the phone number of Dr. Rosen, a friend's marital therapist in New York. My friend had written it on a scrap of paper for me only a week earlier, when I confided that sometimes I felt scarily disconnected from Jeff.

The following day Jeff and I dropped the girls at my cousin's nearby house and drove into the city to see Dr. Rosen. She instructed that Jeff and I should seek every opportunity to ask each other, "How does that make you feel?" which opened up a whole new communication, even though at first it felt awkward, like we were self-help zealots getting in touch with our feelings, a tendency to which I confess being prone.

Acknowledging all that was wrong between us ignited in me this euphoria. I began to believe I had the best of all worlds: living with someone who felt like a new lover, yet someone who had shared my bed for nearly two decades. Sex on week nights. No shy silences. Not having to become accustomed to a new person's bathroom procedures.

I was actually glad this whole thing happened; but then I asked Jeff whether he was glad too and he said, "No." After that, I kept wondering what was going on in his head. One night we took the girls to see *Les Misérables*. While Éponine sang "On My Own," I turned to look at Jeff, so handsome in his navy blazer, suntan, and silver hair. Yet I was sure he was thinking, not of me, but of the woman he had been with, who was now "on her own."

Over the next year, Jeff and I worked on repairing our marriage. The day after we returned to Washington from the beach, we went to Barnes & Noble where we sat in a psychology aisle digging through books for answers to the question, *How do you regain trust?* We also hired a baby sitter for the two days each week I now planned to accompany Jeff to New York.

Sweet memories linger of those times in New York. We stayed at boutique hotels, enjoyed romantic dinners at which I would order a plate of green beans that I couldn't finish (my stomach was not recovering as swiftly as the rest of me), and went to therapy. I rented a locker for the season at the Rockefeller Center ice rink, where I skated while Jeff worked.

One January evening, on the Delta shuttle back to D.C., I said something that must have sounded like legalese, because it led Jeff to ask in an incredulous voice, "Did you go to a lawyer?"

"Yes," I replied. Of course I had gone to a lawyer, given

that I knew divorce was a possibility. I wanted to get an idea of how that worked. Jeff became inconsolable. All that night, he kept turning to me and saying, "You went sneaking off to see a lawyer?"

I thought, Is he crazy? *Does he not get that I went sneaking off to see a lawyer because he had gone sneaking off to be with another woman?*

I asked what he would advise his daughters to do if someday they were to find themselves in my situation. However, nothing I said could calm him down. I actually get it now. He was honestly committed to reforming, wiping the slate to start anew, exposing himself raw in therapy, giving detailed answers to every question. So he must have felt terribly violated that I went to a lawyer without telling him.

After Jeff's revelation about my having seen a lawyer, my ruminating flared up. I worried he would drift again, and I did not want to risk getting infected with HIV or anything else. Nor would I settle for a sexless marriage.

I became obsessed with rifling through Jeff's stuff whenever he wasn't home. Every time I turned up an old credit card statement that showed an expensive dinner a thrill shot through me like the one I remembered from my winning bid of sixty dollars at an auction house for Saul's and my orange sofa. Except now the thrill was from the find; there was no sofa, no prize.

One morning I hit the jackpot when a search of Jeff's gym bag revealed a set of Medeco keys that resembled the ones we'd had when we lived in a New York walk-up apartment. Suspecting Jeff was seeing his girlfriend again, I had to act fast before Jeff returned. I sped in my car to a hardware store that I knew was able to copy security keys.

From there I went to FedEx to overnight the keys to a friend in Manhattan. The following day, she went to the address I gave from the green Post-it on our fridge. Sure enough the keys fit the lock. I waited until our next therapy appointment to confront Jeff. He admitted seeing his girlfriend again, but he wanted another chance.

A friend's words haunted me. *How can you be married to someone you don't trust?* Yet sometimes we got along so well that it felt absurd to be considering divorce. Other times, my rage welled up in the form of daydreams about taking a pair of scissors to his cashmere crewnecks and putting Nair in his Rogaine. And worse. I told my psychiatrist, Dr. Greenberg, about my recurring imagined attacks on Jeff's insides with a steak knife and, naturally, cutting off his penis. Dr. G said this was not a good idea and that I should stop with the cutting fantasies. After that I did stop, which helped to calm my anger.

Double sessions with Jeff in the marital therapist's office, cozy evenings in adorable bistros, intimate overnights on clean hotel sheets, and the synergy of two A-types, who had achieved nearly every goal they had ever set, were not enough to salvage our union. At last, Jeff and I went for a final walk in our neighborhood to discuss how we would tell the kids we were getting divorced. He begged me to reconsider. In the middle of the street in front of our home, we stood sobbing in each other's arms and then went into the house to summon our daughters to the living room. I was not despairing to be losing him. I had made my decision. My tears shed for my little girls' hearts, about to be slit open by a blade whose handle, in our final joint gesture, Jeff and I would grasp, just as we had placed hand over hand to slice our wedding cake eighteen years earlier.

The next day we ate our family meals as usual, talking and laughing as usual, one or two kids crying as usual. It felt so right that Jeff and I looked at each other and asked, "What are we doing? Are we making a mistake?" We made a therapy appointment.

We hashed out with Dr. Kent, our latest psychotherapist, as we had several times before, how we might give our marriage another try. Afterwards, I asked Jeff whether he still thought about his girlfriend, even though he had stopped seeing her. He admitted that he did think about her, and without further analysis, I told myself, *Okay, this is really the end.*

Looking back now, it reminds me of my reaction thirty-two years earlier when my first husband, Saul, told me he had thoughts of his former girlfriend, which promptly hurled me back into Luke's arms and, a few months later, out of my marriage to Saul.

Jeff and I returned home from Dr. Kent's office and I began to pack up everything I owned to the sad news that Princess Diana had died. A few days later Jeff helped me supervise the movers, and he accompanied the girls and me a half-mile away to the house we had originally all planned to move into together. Jeff and I remained congenial enough, until we didn't. One night he told the kids they would be sleeping over at his place, but he hadn't discussed it with me. I flew about in a Rumpelstiltskin rage that led Jeff to proclaim, "I may have ruined the marriage, but you're ruining the divorce."

I spent that year writing daily faxes to my lawyer about every exchange with Jeff. The lawyer suggested we work out custody arrangements with Dr. Kent. She had now become our post-marital therapist, providing us with a safe space for airing our hostilities. We fought hard, not only for each day with the kids, but also for each hour. Given the choice at the time, I would not have shared the kids with him for a minute, but now I admire him for having insisted on nine consecutive days with them, during which time our girls formed a bond with their dad, perhaps even stronger than they might have if Jeff and I had stayed married.

Jeff and I continued to go to our children's soccer games, where we sat together, chatting like a pair of soccer moms. Other parents remarked that it was hard to believe we were divorced.

Over the years I have played and replayed the what-ifs. *What if I had never found out? Wouldn't my life have been just fine? What if I had given it more time? Would we have stayed together? What if we had stayed together? Would I have always wondered what he was up to? Would he have divorced me after the last kid graduated high school? Did I love him enough? Did I love him at all? Should I have arranged romantic vacations and been more willing to leave the girls? If we had stayed together, would my life be better or worse than it is now? Would we have grown closer or remained distant? I would never have had a dog.*

DIVORCED
WITH KIDS

SINGLE MOM
1997–1998

Even before learning about Jeff's girlfriend, I felt a grow-ing distance between him and me. In the health club locker room—amid women in various states of undress—I would get this urge to shout, "Plane Crash Fantasy!" just to see how many pairs of knowing eyes would look my way.

As during my single years, when I had wished my parents dead, the fantasy entailed a swift conclusion for Jeff, whose passport was as thick as a paperback novel. A jet malfunction somewhere off the coast of Japan perhaps. Yet when I heard on the radio that an aircraft went down near Shanghai, where Jeff was traveling, the degree to which my stomach churned assured me of what I already knew: that of course I did not really want my children's father to die.

The plane crash fantasy had been my way, more dignified than an illicit affair, to make room for romance with an

163

imaginary stranger, who would thrill me with caresses as lost to the past as my prom-queen skin tone. Despite the daydream of becoming uncoupled, the first moments the massive crevice in my marriage became obvious, I wished that—as happens with a near-death experience—I could return to my normal life. I had been living with deep fissures for longer than I'd realized, the way you notice plaster bubbling all over your bathroom ceiling one day because you happened to stretch out on the floor to do sit ups. You showered there every night, knew there were some puckers, but had no idea the extent of the damage.

After my separation, I understood why people's faces acquired a silent scream look as they unwound from their marriages. But every so often I spotted an attractive man, and a spark crackled that made my hollow eyes shine at the prospect of serial romances like those I'd had in my twenties. I remembered how it felt to step into a restaurant and have men look up from their soup. Now, however, when I walked into Starbucks for my morning coffee, men's faces remained fastened to their *Wall Street Journals*.

During those early, teary, post-separation weeks with my children, just the four of us in the basement of our new house while the upstairs was being remodeled, I had more to worry about than finding a love interest. Managing a renovation and a divorce simultaneously had the potential to overwhelm my long waking hours with anxiety. So I found a way to spin this double load I was dealing with. For instance, when Jeff scolded me for getting back to his house late from an after-school date with one of our daughters, I stared into his mahogany eyes and thought about the wrong shade of green the painters had applied earlier that day to my bathroom walls, which made me feel better. Having a worry duo appealed to my pragmatic side.

Without a husband, I sought men to look after me: my lawyer, my psychiatrist, a boy dog. There were also around fifty workers at a large house being gutted across the street. After my own muddy-booted crew had packed up for good, my neighbor's workmen helped me with everything from erecting a doggie run to reassuring me that mounds of tiny shavings in my storage closet were not from termites.

I remarked to a friend, "If I don't have a fling with one of those construction guys, I ought to consider myself a failure." The idea seemed convenient and uncomplicated, as though this were the seventies and my marriage had been nothing more than a long dream. In my traumatic stupor, I was not sure whether I intended my casual sex remark as a quip. Nor was I certain that I could take full responsibility for my actions, as I wobbled to and fro between my role of mother and my role of imagined seductress.

Regardless, I did not have to answer to anyone about what took place in my head, which was where I feared my romantic ruminations would have to remain, since the how-to-divorce books commanded me to set an example for my daughters. I wondered whether I could wait a decade, till my youngest was off to college, to get involved with a man. By then it might be too late to attract someone who still had his original teeth.

Only one among the construction crew captured my fancy. Ron, the project manager, was trim with short, salt-and-pepper hair and a ready grin that gave him the chronic appearance of a schoolboy who had just gotten into mischief, which was what I liked about him. Whenever I passed the window on my stair landing, I peeked between the sheer curtains to see if I could catch a glimpse of him.

Sometimes I lined my eyes, rouged my cheeks, tucked my turtleneck into my jeans, and walked over with a plate of cookies for the workmen. What I really had in mind was to get Ron to notice me. Ron's friendly but limited response spun my brain into explanations. *He must think it would be unprofessional to make a pass at me, womanizing on the job. He must have a girlfriend.* And the old standby, *maybe he's gay.* I dismissed the notion that he was just not interested. Then I invited him to my divorce party and he said he would let me know, but he never did, which alerted me that I was now fifty-two-year-old Susan Orlins, no longer twenty-five-year-old Susan Fishman.

THE DIVORCE PARTY
1998

For a while we pondered whether to take a vacation or get a divorce. We decided a trip to Bermuda is over in two weeks, but a divorce is something you always have.   —WOODY ALLEN

Newly divorced, I swung from thinking every man who captured my interest would ask me out to believing I would never have another date. Worried, I decided to throw myself a divorce party.

The last time I'd had a singles party, Jimmy Carter was President, no one had ever heard of date rape, and I had just moved back to D.C. from Vermont after being fired from my job as a hatcheck girl at the Sirloin Saloon, because a coat was stolen when I left early (with permission) to catch a bus to New York to visit my boyfriend, Elliott, who dumped me the following week.

My divorce party invitation list totalled eleven: three former beaus and eight unattached women. So I solicited married friends for names of AARP card-carrying singles. On each phone call, I explained that the event would be potluck and then I asked, "Who else should I invite?" One guy wanted to bring his whole Jewish singles dinner club. Curious married friends begged to come and serve.

Next to each name I made notes: *goes to psychic, grew up on a reservation, dentist.*

Yikes, now I had to plan a party!

As soon as twenty men and twenty women accepted, I stopped inviting. And started worrying. Maybe no one would show. Or everyone would show at the exact same moment. Someone could trip over a lamp cord. What if singles got into car crashes on the way? It would be my fault for having invited them. What's more, I had heard about robberies at parties where everyone had to strip and hand over their watches.

Actually the strip and rob scenario didn't sound so bad; at least it wouldn't be boring. On party day I became consumed with fear that no one would talk, convinced I would have the first totally silent social gathering in history. To distract myself, I latched onto another obsession: people could get potluck food poisoning.

Party night arrived and doubts continued. Was my outfit too sexy? Was it sexy enough? Remarkably, guests arrived evenly-spaced, everyone mingled, and no one tripped. The only low moment occurred when I was chatting with my pal Alice and a lawyer named Will, who had the square jaw of a football player and whom thirty years earlier I had dated once or twice.

He asked Alice, "Did you know Susan Fishman in her twenties? She was so exotic."

His comment would have been okay, even flattering, if I had been able to accept just how exotic I, now Susan Orlins, was not at this newly-divorced re-encounter. What did he mean by exotic anyway?

Will's remark notwithstanding, a few nights later a charming fellow from the party named Peter phoned and asked me out. My first post-divorce date! He wanted to know what time he should pick me up. I replied, "With my daughters living at home, I think I should meet you somewhere."

Now get ready for the rest of what I said to this virtual stranger, "When we're engaged, you can pick me up."

If you have never gone through a divorce, let me propose you prepare for this kind of gut-flip-flopping, bile-choking, brain-exploding remark to just fall out of your mouth without warning. Peter was decent enough not to break the date. Instead, we had dinner at his place where he had assembled a protective layer of friends.

I continued to give singles parties, though I wonder what masochistic bent drove me to entertain, given how it terrified me and still does. Some people hang-glide; I host. It must satisfy my craving to live on the edge.

LOSING THE CUTE MAN
1998

Cutie arrived in the early eighties, shortly after Eliza
was born. For a decade he dwelled in a toy chest with
other nameless bears until he was adopted by Sabrina, who
herself had been adopted at birth. Cutie attended piano lessons, rode swings, and served as ringmaster under the big top
into which Sabrina and her two sisters had converted our living room.

And when their father and I summoned our girls to that
same room to tell them we were getting divorced, Cutie came
too, squeezed in Sabrina's arms as she rocked and keened in a
corner of the couch. Just as I had never imagined our dinner
table reduced to a permanent foursome, it never occurred to
me that there might be a time without Cutie.

On our third winter holiday as a reconfigured family, I
landed at Heathrow with Eliza, Sabrina, and Emily—ages six-

teen, twelve, and ten—for a four-day vacation. "Make sure we don't leave anything, Em," I said to my youngest, as I undid my seatbelt and wedged guidebooks into my overstuffed tote.

It was at baggage claim that I noticed Sabrina oddly empty-handed. "Where's Cutie?" I asked.

Her lips formed a silent O, as if to say oops.

"Wait here," I called to the others. I grabbed Sabrina's hand and ran to the nearby customer service desk. On the missing property form, I wrote: *bear, grayish, approx twelve inches, under seat 45H.*

"It's there. Now. Can't you do something?" I pleaded with the man in blue. He handed me a card and said, "Ring this number later. They'll tell you if they've found it."

I had to think fast. Something told me to personally rescue The Cute Man, as I sometimes called him, but Eliza would no doubt be sprinting over momentarily to say she had the bags; I pictured her with eyes narrowing, urging us to hurry. Plus, having spent roughly three hours planning for every hour we would be in London, I was deeply invested in the success of our mini trip—the *Reader's Digest* condensed version of a family vacation—competing with the week, including Christmas, the children would be spending in the Caribbean with their father. Because I selfishly did not want this inauspicious beginning to spoil our first day, I rationalized that with such specific information someone would surely find Cutie. Nonetheless, as we pulled away from the airport, my stomach churned.

Each morning, while the children slept, I tiptoed out of our room to phone British Airways. And each time an indifferent voice informed me no such bear had turned up, I winced, as though a dart were sailing toward the bridge of my nose and I stood nightmarishly frozen, unable to duck. Each evening when I tucked in Sabrina and kissed her forehead, she asked, "Do you think we'll find Cutie?"

"I hope so" the first night became "Maybe not" by the eve of our departure.

As prospects for finding Cutie dimmed, there was no avoiding self-accusations. I knew that the toys, sweaters, and backpacks my children had left behind over the years could have outfitted a whole village of young girls; I, the mother, should have searched under our seats instead of delegating to Emily. If it had been my laptop, I would have run back to the plane, which was what I should have done despite Eliza's objections, which were all in my imagination anyway. More guilt. Sabrina's loss made me think about all of her losses: being separated from her birth mother, having her parents divorce and, now, losing The Cute Man.

When we returned to the airport for our flight home, through sheer determination, I planned to track down Cutie. A uniformed woman led Sabrina and me with a brisk swagger down a tunnel-like corridor to a counter behind which stood dozens of suitcases on rows of shelves. I craned my neck, hoping to glimpse a grayish tuft among the bags. "We're looking for my daughter's bear that we left on a plane four days ago," I told the lost-and-found attendant. "I can give you our exact seat number."

"Sorry, you need to talk to the company we've subcontracted that to," he said as he dialed and handed me the phone.

After I repeated my story, the voice in charge of missing bears replied, "No, we have nothing like that here."

I gazed down at Sabrina and shook my head. Her face crumpled and she began to cry soundlessly. I wrapped my arms around her slender torso and through my own tears said, "I'm sorry, Baby. I'm so sorry."

No one mentioned Cutie for a long time, except Eliza, who wanted to know why I hadn't cried when someone at her nursery school, years earlier, had swiped Big Pete. "Big Pete wasn't a family member," I said with as much gentleness as I could muster; I was absorbed in thought, recollecting the night in our kitchen just days before when we all danced the hora—Sabrina and Eliza each holding a Cutie paw—and sang by the light of our menorah.

After we returned to the rhythm of our lives, I kept trying to accept that I would never again see Sabrina hug The Cute Man. At a post-Christmas sale, I bought a replacement teddy whose legs, Sabrina pointed out, were attached in the wrong place. My attempts to dance this no-name stranger into the bedtime ritual seemed only to heighten the sense of loss.

Knowing that no matter how intensely I mourned, I could not absorb my daughter's pain, I wondered to what extent my own losses were masquerading as grief for Cutie. Each month my world shattered anew when my children packed stuffed bears and pajamas and moved two miles away to their father's house for nine days, while I wobbled on the rim of a black hole before catching my balance. Having to reinvent myself after ending my marriage to a man who, for nearly twenty years, had called *me* Cutie—was my sadness all tangled up with that?

There was also the obvious symbolism: a daughter on the cusp of adolescence loses her favorite stuffed animal. Perhaps I never recovered from having to surrender my own childhood and from the fact that my children, who had fit so neatly into those parts of me that refused to grow up, were moving on, leaving me abandoned, like Cutie.

One night, Sabrina plucked from her shelf Pat the Bunny whose coat was the color of ashes, like The Cute Man's. "Pat smells just like Cutie," she remarked, which seemed to soothe her. I had been yammering something about regret, and Sabrina said, "You know what I regret?" She must have seen on my face the compassion that welled up inside me when she said, "No, Mom, it's not Cutie. It's that I decided not to have a birthday party this year." It was her matter-of-fact air that jolted me into believing she had come to terms with Cutie's fate.

Now I would try to do the same.

With trepidation, I sent this chapter to Sabrina to see whether including it in my book would upset her. She replied, "Awww Mom this is sweet! It doesn't make me sad anymore, more sad that YOU were so sad by it! Cutie's probably fully English now, sipping a 'cuppa.'"

THE MATCHMAKER
2000

"A matchmaker?" I groaned when a friend told me I had to try Leora. I had visions of *Fiddler on the Roof*—Yenta, her hair tucked into a babushka, introducing me to a butcher. Even though every pore in my body argued against it, I knew my curiosity would obliterate good judgment. Subjecting myself to new gimmicks for meeting men was as inescapable as sampling every dish at a buffet—synthetic bacon bits from the salad bar, gray meat afloat in cornstarch gravy, and cherry Jell-O cubes below Dream Whip peaks.

If this had been Jane Austen's nineteenth-century England, I might have been able to rely on friends or relatives to alert potential suitors of my availability and to introduce me to such men at a ball. Instead, as a fifty-two-year-old neophyte divorcée, I had found romance with an old friend, which allowed me to believe there would be a man in my future to hold my hand during cataract surgery.

175

After I became overly eager, suggesting we get together twice in one week, Old Friend lost interest. I then began and ended a second relationship, opting for the pain of losing my beau to the anxiety of wondering when he was going to call. It was not as easy as I'd figured it might be to pick up where I had left off when I met Jeff two decades earlier: in my twenties, finding men with good smiles was easy. Now, however, those Good Smiles were inching toward Medicare eligibility; most wore wedding bands; and the bare-fingered ones were not flashing their bleached cuspids at my somewhat pleasant, but lined and sagging face. If only they knew how many boys had had crushes on me in high school, but I guess Marlon Brando had once been a heart-stopper too.

So there I was with my calendar wide open, available to socialize with other subscribers to singles@kosher.com, which e-mailed a weekly smorgasbord of events to Jewish unmarrieds: Nosh and Groove Jazz Brunch, Shabbat Dinner Italiana, Gefilte Fish Gala. Every holiday presented its own mixer opportunity, such as Purimpalooza Happy Hour. It wasn't that I cared whether I noshed with men who had been bar mitzvah boys or whether I salsa danced with señors who knew what *muchos besos* meant; I simply liked that this website offered the possibility of meeting someone new every night of the week. Just knowing there was somewhere to go felt more hopeful, less lonely.

Characteristically, I tried each event once until the sameness of these gatherings made me feel trapped in a museum-like video, playing and rewinding, playing and rewinding. Chicken wings, carrot sticks, chips, chicken wings, carrot sticks, chips, unless I arrived late, and then there were just the chips. The occasional attractive guy my age always seemed to be hunched in conversation with a blonde whose neck was as smooth as a Pinot Grigio bottle, while men closer to my father's age than mine gazed into my concealer-rimmed eyes and droned on about volunteering at the zoo and other retirement time fillers, which made me consider signing up for an Elderhostel trip, so I could be the babe.

It was a numbers game. The more places I went, the more dates I generated, an average of one date from every three events. Although I did my best to be my own cheerleader, my self-image was shaky, and mingling with elderly singles made me feel old by association. The young never-marrieds made me feel old by contrast. When it finally occurred to me that the likelihood of meeting someone arresting during these gatherings was slim, and that I would be far more content alone in a movie theater, I stopped going.

Feeling battered by the guys who never approached me, and lacking the patience to sit around and wait for a man who was not materializing, I stopped caring whether a fellow with hairy legs was sharing my bed. In fact, I began to believe that sharing my bed with my hairy beagle was at least as pleasurable and a lot less bother. So when I phoned Leora the matchmaker, it was from a position of indifference, which I considered to be a position of strength.

Leora told me, "We'll get together for an initial meeting. Then we'll decide if we want to work together. There's no obligation."

No commitment, I liked that. I suggested she come to my home, figuring that on my own turf I could impress her with a show and tell performance—some of my published essays, the paint by number canvases my teenage daughters and I had started the previous summer, and the photo album from my homecoming queen years (well, I was never actually nominated to be homecoming queen). Leora would get to know the real me.

Preparing to meet Leora turned out to be as intense as primping for a prom, because despite my claims of nonchalance, somewhere inside me lived a little girl's dream of meeting a prince. The better the impression I could make on Leora, the better the matches she would make for me. So there I was on a sunny Monday morning, blow drying my hair and applying "caramel" eye color to my brow bone. I had Naired the fine hairs along my jaw the night before. My decision to neaten up the living room waylaid my plan to shower. After spraying the house with Clean Sheets, an air freshener that smells like its name, I spritzed a final misty cloud and stepped into it.

Smelling fresh as a newly-made bed, I opened the door to meet my matchmaker. Instead of the confident, straight-backed businesswoman wearing a serious suit, brown pumps, and flawless manicure—whom I pictured once I had gotten past the Yenta image—on my stoop stood a crimped-haired woman sporting the kind of slacks, sweater, and chipped nail polish you see on a soccer mom like me. The instant chemistry I had hoped for was missing; rather, I felt that deflated sensation I remembered from opening the door to a disappointing blind date. Nonetheless, I swept Leora to a seat on the sofa and, with Miss America charm, offered her iced tea.

Given how I delighted in questions that allowed me to talk about myself, I decided it would endear me to Leora if I asked how she came to be a matchmaker. A half-hour later I was still listening, impatiently waiting for her to ask about *moi*, which, as you can imagine, would have improved her odds of winning me as a client.

Before leaving, Leora outlined three levels of what she called "investing in the membership," as though this were a country club. For five hundred dollars a year, she would supply introductions from her "pool" of members; for twenty-five hundred dollars, Leora would venture outside of her pool to headhunt Mr. Right, running personal ads and attending singles events (the same dreary ones I had stopped going to); and for five thousand dollars she would provide "Executive Search Membership," which included psychological tests and "best efforts."

"Who would pay five thousand dollars?" I asked.

"Well, for example," she said, "I have a twenty-five-year-old client who is a virgin and has never had a girlfriend. His mother paid the fee."

Leora handed me a folder containing legal documents and an eleven-page questionnaire, which included inquiries about psychotherapy and criminal records. If I signed up, would she fingerprint me? Would I have to tell about my brush with the law in 1971 when a policeman escorted me into custody from the community college classroom where I was teaching statistics, because I refused to sign a summons for parking one-third of my VW in a campus no-parking zone? I was glad at least that she would sift out of her pool any grand larcenists before fixing me up.

As she was leaving, Leora mentioned that as part of the service she would tell a guy if I didn't want to see him again. Given my anxiety about inflicting rejection, having someone to undo my matches, I thought, would be the best thing about having a matchmaker.

My objection to paying for the opportunity to meet a man who had also paid to meet me, rather than waiting for a chance encounter at, say, the dry cleaner, was always the same. What loser guy would pay to meet a woman? My double standard that women do this kind of thing allowed me to overlook my own loser status. Plus, no one knew any unattached middle-aged men, but everyone knew dozens of single women.

A week after our meeting, Leora phoned. "Hi Sue," she said with an unwise attempt at intimacy, using a moniker I disowned when I reinvented myself after high school. "I have two men in mind for you, if you are planning to sign up." Compelling if I cared as deeply as I had during that optimistic first year after my separation but, in any case, an attention getter.

"The first is a very nice guy. He designs jewelry store windows." An artist. I liked that. "He's good-looking and wears designer clothes. Oh, and he has a beard. I don't know how you feel about facial hair. The only problem is, he's tall." I had told her I like a man who is in touch with his female side, which she apparently interpreted to exclude basketball players. "He doesn't have kids, lives about a forty-minute drive from you, and his name is Herb."

She paused, which I took as my cue to critique Herb. "I like that his job is a little different. Tall is okay, but I'm worried about the designer clothes. And I have never been attracted to someone who would live that far from the city."

After dismissing the designer clothes as nothing (did she mean "designer clothes" referred to Polo shirts rather than Armani suits?), she said, "He wants to move. And anyway, no one's perfect. You have to prioritize your issues."

So I decided not to tell her how hard it was to imagine liking someone named Herb. I know this seems shallow, but I dredged up all the Herbs I could think of. There was the singer Herb of Peaches and Herb. And President Herb Hoover. My former husband's former boss at the State De-

partment, the former legal advisor, Herb Hansel. And finally, Herb Herman, my parents' friend who in the fifties, sold
girls' coordinates from his basement and outfitted me in full
skirts imprinted with tiny rosebuds and matching seersucker
sleeveless blouses.

I was not thinking there were no suitable Herbs out there,
it was just that I had not met any; the percentages were not in
Herb's favor. Actually, Herb Herman was attractive for someone my father's age. Maybe if you took his looks, Herb Hansel's
intellect, Herb Hoover's presidential status, and Peaches and
Herb's Herb's talent and combined them, you would have one
very fine Herb. But Leora's double-breasted Herb, to whom a
visit would entail traveling on a high-speed thoroughfare, was
not what I had in mind. As for H names, something more in
the way of a Harrison (Ford, in blue jeans) suited me better.

The second candidate was named Jeff, same as the husband I had divorced. Ever since, I have thought how weird
it would be to land in bed beside another Jeff. "Oh, Jeff, Jeff,
more, more . . ." I have my doubts about another Jeff, although
this one, unlike my last Jeff, was a good dancer. In fact, Leora
told me twice what a good dancer he was, which made me
think that a smooth rumba was the main thing he had going
for him. Instead, I wished she had told me he subscribed to
The New Yorker.

Like Herb, Jeff lived too far to be anywhere near the peak
of my bell curve of likely prospects. Leora advised me (her advice is also part of the service) to "strike while the iron's hot,"
as though she were giving me first dibs, jumping the lineup of
women who were about to snatch Herb and Jeff if I hesitated.
It surprised me that, rather than just tweaking my curiosity,
Leora had provided me with these two resumes even though I

had not agreed to become a member of her pool.

I told Leora that I would consider signing up but that I was pretty busy for the rest of the month. What I was thinking was that Herb and Jeff were the gray meat and cherry Jell-O of Leora's smorgasbord, that they had paid her thousands of dollars to recruit dates for them, and that perhaps Leora needed me more than I needed her.

The following morning I met two friends, Evie and Madeline, for coffee. If my own reservations were not enough to put the Herb matter to rest, when I told the story of Leora and Herb, Madeline said, "It doesn't sound like he's for you. He lives too far." Evie said, "And what's with the name Herb?"

Weeks went by and I had not heard from Leora. Was that it? Was she dumping me? I was still dying to try matchmaking. I daydreamed I'd take out an ad: DWF seeks mtchmkr w/gd manicure, no pickups frm singles@kosher.com, cnvnient zip codes, no Hrbs.

Or that I would sign up with Valenti International, *Matchmaking in the European Tradition*, whose advertisement I had torn from an airline magazine. The full-page spread featured a color photograph of Irene Valenti, president, ambiguously stepping into or out of a red convertible. A gorgeous blonde, she looked ageless, wearing an obviously pricey cream-colored collarless suit that exposed a vee of smooth, tan skin from chin to cleavage. Her nails were polished to a high shine. The text boasted a select worldwide clientele. Although Herb and Jeff lived too far, a mate domiciled in Chicago, Montreal, or Paris sounded just right, so I would be able to continue wallowing in the solitude to which I had grown accustomed.

THE "FAMILY VACATION"
2004 - 2012

"The whole family's in the pool," Eliza called out in a tone as sparkly as the cool water after I eased in to join the three girls and Jeff.

It was the summer of 2004, six years after Jeff's and my divorce became final. Emily, Sabrina, and Eliza were sixteen, seventeen and twenty-one; camps, trips, and jobs allowed only nine days that we were all available at the same time. Jeff phoned me to discuss how to divvy up the time.

I searched my mind for a way to get five days to his four.

But then I had an inspiration and suggested that rather than each of us taking a mini holiday with the kids, all five of us could go away together for twice as long.

Jeff agreed.

The novelty alone pleased me. Plus, Jeff and I had recovered sufficiently from the bruises of our union and its dissolution. We both had new love interests; neither of us was pining for the other.

Even during the worst moments since the divorce, we had managed to compartmentalize our differences and solve problems whenever issues arose regarding the girls. In fact, I was often secretly grateful for a crisis, so I could experience the fuzzy feeling of good will between Jeff and me.

As soon as I entered our East Hampton rental house on that first day of the first family vacation, I scurried to check out bedrooms and stake claim to the one with the most windows. Jeff cared about quiet; I cared about openings to the outdoors. He was happiest in a room away from the kitchen and girls' rooms; I liked the sorority atmosphere of a room near the kids. Jeff avoided bickering; I was a better bickerer.

I bickered better and got the bedroom farthest from the kitchen and the only one with a door to the outside. Jeff ended up in the room closest to the kitchen and the morning rumpus.

Breakfast was one of my favorite parts of the day. Jeff brewed coffee, while I biked to get *The New York Times* and fresh bread. He and I would then sit on the deck with the paper, sipping coffee and chatting about politics. One by one the girls straggled out with eggs and bowls of fruit. Then we all shared stories from our laptops or the newspaper. One of the things I missed most after Jeff and I separated was reading *The Times* with him.

Every day we went to the beach no matter what. Jeff had Weatherman in his DNA and sometimes he had us head out while it was raining, and then by the time we stepped onto the sand with our folding chairs, the sun would be peeking through as he'd predicted.

On such weather days we were practically the only ones at the water's edge. Though all alike in our fondness for sleeping on blankets and reading, everyone except me loved going in the ocean. I disliked the feeling of water on my face and was afraid of waves. Whenever they went on long swims, I alerted the lifeguards, "See those four dots out there, that's my family. Would you mind keeping an eye on them?"

At night we chopped, peeled, grilled, and sautéed, rarely venturing into the village, which was dense with city folks wearing sports clothes, like those sold at a shop called Cashmere Hampton. We headed out only when we wanted to prowl the bookstore, get ice cream cones, or see a movie.

Sometimes during dinner Jeff and I told stories about our pre-marriage years. One of Jeff's favorites took place while we were still dating. On warm Friday evenings, he and I frequently squeezed onto a Long Island Railroad car to spend summer weekends with his parents. On one such trip a muffled siren began to blare. I turned to Jeff and shouted, "Sounds like someone's portable smoke alarm has gone off."

At this point in the story I took over and told how his incredulous look had made clear he'd found the suggestion preposterous that anyone besides me had packed a travel smoke alarm. In any case, from then on I always removed the alarm's batteries before placing it in my wheelie bag.

After dinner we would line up in front of the TV, each of us with a laptop balanced on our thighs. It was the 2004 Olympics and Jeff and the girls liked seeing the competitions. Jeff got teary watching mini-documentaries of athletes' personal struggles as well as unexpected victories and heartbreaking losses.

I didn't mind having the Olympics on, though it made me sad to see kids packaged into mono-track lives that deprived them of their childhoods. No one agreed with me; I was the sole Debbie Downer when it came to the Olympics.

Recently we completed our third Olympics cycle, our

ninth consecutive family vacation. I love not being the only one responsible for everyone's fun, and each year reinforces our family bond.

Once, however, Jeff got really angry with me. He berated me because he thought I was behind a plan to watch a three-hour episode of *The Bachelor,* which occurred the evening Emily had arrived, and it forced us to race through dinner.

Then there was the summer Jeff asked how I felt about his girlfriend, Nan, coming for the weekend. My daughters had already heard rumblings about this, so I had anticipated the question. I figured it would be a new experience and if it turned out not to be fun, at least it would be a good story to write about.

Apparently the weekend began on Thursday morning, as that was when Nan arrived. For dinner that night she whipped up a tasty veggie soup, using whatever produce was sitting around, going wrinkly.

After eating we gathered in front of the TV to watch the DVD I had rented, a documentary called *Harvard Beats Yale 29-29*. Jeff had been at that 1968 football game.

Jeff was the first to lower himself to the floor to do back stretches. I joined him, the way I ordinarily did. It economized on time to stretch while watching a movie. As we had done side-by-side every night for the eighteen years of our marriage, Jeff and I pulled knees to chest and pressed spines to the floor in tandem. Something about this routine felt intimate in a familiar, not romantic, way that made me wonder how it made Nan feel.

One by one heads flopped to this side or that. Soon, slumber sounds of three daughters and one girlfriend hummed in the background.

When the movie ended, the others woke up and said what

an awful choice that had been. Jeff sat between Nan's feet so she could massage his neck. The rest of us tapped on our laptops. I didn't want to be the one massaging Jeff's neck—I had a guy in Washington with a neck—but now I was the one feeling a territorial twinge, in this case, about Jeff's neck.

Finally Jeff and Nan headed upstairs to his room, and shortly thereafter the girls and I went downstairs to our rooms in the kids' wing.

On the beach the following day the three girls and I rigged up the timer on Eliza's digital camera to take jumping photos. Each time after the camera clicked, we ran to look at the picture of our arms stretched skyward, fingers splayed, faces contorted, backs arched, legs all about. And each time we crumbled with laughter.

Meanwhile Jeff and Nan sat off to the side in beach chairs, reading with sober faces, their matching wet suits drying on their chair backs.

A few weeks after the vacation ended, I reported to my cognitive therapist that Nan and I had hardly exchanged words. Having her there, I thought, altered the chemistry for everyone, not least of all for Jeff.

Cognitive Therapist replied, "It's a bad idea, Susan, to go along with something like the Nan visit, just because it might provide fodder for your blog." I never did write about it.

So when it's only "the family" is it perfect? No. We suck at rainy days, flopping all over the couch with our laptops. And, as in any family, sometimes the girls squabble. Whenever they do, I roll my eyes at Jeff who rolls his eyes back at me in a moment of shared parenting. The only thing odd about our nine-day vacation, is that it feels so normal to all be together.

Worrywart as Jewish Mother To A Stranger

2011

Recently in New York I saw a flier stapled to a telephone pole that said:

Sarah

Needs

A

Job

.com

I was so intrigued by this that I went to Sarah's website. Sarah Feldman is around the age of my daughters, and I thought I could help, so I e-mailed her.

On Sunday, Mar 27, 2011 at 5:03 PM, Susan Orlins wrote:

Hi Sarah. I saw your flier and loved it. Went back to photograph it for my blog www.confessionsofaworrywart.com. But someone had taken down the ones I'd seen. I was intrigued, because I thought your fliers showed great initiative and imagination.

I also like your website, though as a mother of 3 girls in their 20s, I wanted to make a couple of motherly suggestions.

I apologize in advance for being presumptuous.

One, I would clean up any language you can, because I think it won't appeal to employers. I would remove the f-word, even from comments and I would rename your NEWYORKSHITTY page.

I love how your enthusiasm comes through and if I were an employer, I would be inspired to interview you, but also I would be a bit put off by the angry tone that shows up... naturally you feel that way. Maybe there's a humorous or other way to express it.

Anyway, all that said, I'd like to mention you on my blog and maybe at some point do a separate post about you.

Oh, one more thing. I couldn't tell what you do? I think from a comment that you are an artist and went to Pratt. It would be nice to know that. I adore the graphic on your homepage and the earrings you make!!

Good luck and I hope to hear from you and I hope you take my suggestions as coming from a well-meaning (overbearing Jewish) mother.

Labohemianartist, aka Sarah, replied:
newyorkshitty.com isn't my website.

How Annoying Am I?
1997 - 2012

R*epeating Myself.* "Mom, you told me that ten times!"

Asking Too Many Questions. Just after exchanging "I love yous" and "mwahs" at the end of a phone conversation, a string of questions spills out of my mouth like bubbles from a wand:
"What are you up to later?"
"Did you get your exam back?"
"By the way, is so-and-so doing better?"
You get the idea.

Focusing on Unimportant Details. Even though I'm a writer, my daughters often forsake my counsel on something they are writing, rather than having to put up with my nitpicks.

Going Off on Tangents Rather Than Adhering to Linear Discourse. All three daughters exhibit annoyance with my tangents. "So what happened?" someone will ask. And then I'll say, "blah blah *tangent* blah blah," and then she'll ask, "But what *happened*?" We go back and forth like this for a while until finally she begs, "Can you get to the point?"

Being Too Much of a Problem Solver. The time I bought phyllo dough, which was wrong in the first place because I hadn't known it was different from puff pastry, I also didn't know I needed to defrost it for several hours for the onion tarts Sabrina was planning to make. So I jumped on the Internet and began trying solutions like hot water, the microwave and my own idea of placing it underneath our sleeping beagle, Casey.

Posing Too Many Options. "What should we do? We can bike then play Boggle or play Boggle then bike." To see how annoying I can be, mix bike and Boggle with all the permutations of more options, like watch a movie, do a jigsaw puzzle, walk the dog, read by the fire, paint by number, cook, bake, go to the Shanghainese café . . .

Stalking on Social Networks. When your daughter is in Colombia, South America and has not tweeted all day, is it every mother's tweetmare that her kid is locked in the trunk of a sedan?

Talking Too Much About my Writing and Giving Too Much Advice. I write three articles a week, many that offer advice, so nearly everything relates to something I've written. I try to hold back on my Know-It-All, but still I'm annoying.

Exhibiting Neediness. Say Eliza is coming home to D.C. for the night because an old friend will be coming to town. I point out that it's a weekend, never intending to pressure her, but just in case she hadn't noticed and might want to stay two nights rather than just one night. Exhibiting neediness and being annoying.

Asking, "Am I Being Too Annoying?" Just recently I was in a high-end pizza place with Emily. I asked the waiter where my salad was. He said I hadn't ordered it, which was true, as I'd gotten over-involved in the details of my pizza order (under-cooked, tomatoes on the side, etc.).

I happily said he could bring it any time it was ready. Somewhere in here it seemed he was upset with me, so I tried to be uber-friendly and Emily told me in an uncharacteristically terse tone, "He was laughing at you, not with you." So then I wanted to say something to him to fix it and she told me, "Just stop."

Ordinarily I would ask her, "Am I being too annoying?" but it was so obvious.

Worrying. Sabrina has asked me not to hug her every time she leaves the house in a way that suggests I'll never see her again.

Displaying Absent-Mindedness. When was the last time I didn't have to make a trip from the checkout line to the car for the reusable grocery bags? Never.

Talking Bedbug Talk. Now that I've created a panic about these dreaded insects, I've been banned by my daughters from mentioning the b-word. But sometimes it's imperative to point out a new risk, like after I read they could be hiding in the battery compartment of the TV remote control.

However . . . In defense of my ways, whenever it's possible to self-correct, I do. After asking my daughter if the cool guy she met at a party ever called and she said I was annoying and that she was never going to tell me about anyone ever again, I never asked about anyone again, except maybe once, and so she resumed telling me about this guy and that guy.

DIVORCED WITH DOG

Is My Dog Bored?

2010

When we brought Casey home from the pound in 1999, he looked so woebegone. On the rare occasion that I caught him wagging his tail, I tried to reinforce the behavior, saying, "Good tail, good tail!"

I never gave much thought to whether my passive, yet eager-to-please, little guy suffered from boredom. But now I'm worried.

It started when I returned from a trip and noticed him pawing to get at something under the sofa. Upon closer inspection I discovered a few impossible-to-reach kibbles.

The dog sitter told me, "Oh, I planted those so he wouldn't be bored." The kibbles seemed to frustrate him, so I removed them. But now that it's been pointed out to me, I can't stop thinking how bored Casey looks, except when—like every dog in America—he flies around in circles, howling, as the mailperson rounds the corner onto our block.

Which is not to say Casey hasn't experienced excitement beyond the quotidian mail delivery, excitement such as encounters with a squirrel in our house and a deer in our yard.

And let's call it negative excitement the time he got his head stuck in an empty bag of dog food, which I thought would be a fun plaything for him. Well, it created an air pocket in his stomach, which I thought was a tumor. The two of us sat quaking for hours at the all-night vet after which I had to pay more than it costs for a weekend in Atlantic City.

These adventures have provided my Sweet Potato with an increased heart rate an average of once every four and one-third years, not including when we have company for dinner and he melts into the rug under the table, acting like he's not paying a whit of attention, until someone takes one step away from his plate. Faster than you can say Jack Robinson, Casey whoomps an entire chicken breast into his mouth. What dog wouldn't?

As for interaction with other dogs, Casey is a bully. But he can do tricks. "Come!" challenges him, yet he scoots to my side in a jiffy at the "Come for a treat!" command (hence, one of his nicknames, Scooter Libby). And since he routinely remains motionless, he excels at the "full face or profile" command. On the other hand, he thinks "Fetch!" means watch Mommy throw a ball and yell "Fetch!"

Am I projecting my own fear of boredom onto my furry best friend? At the very least I must own up to my role in Casey's perceived ennui. Thrice a day I walk him across the street. A better master would walk him around the block. Nonetheless, while whippets and puggles are trotting around the neighborhood, my Muffin is home getting smushed with hugs.

In the same way I sometimes "try on" other people's lives

to see how they fit, I "try on" other people's dogs. My friend Francesca has two Labradoodles. They're always flopping around in tandem, up and down the stairs, in and out the doggie door, on and off Francesca's lap. It wears me out to be around them, but I envy the jovial ambience they provide.

Then I return home to my mellow fellow, the living creature with whom I have perhaps shared the most hours of my life, and I go all tranquil. Even when he smells bad, Casey smells scrumptious to me, the way my babies appealed to my olfactory sense, no matter what. And maybe that is part of the point. Loving your dog, even when he's an old man, can feel so much like loving your baby. At bedtime he cradles in my arms like a newborn and I rub his tummy before we drift off to sleep.

Though Casey's eyes are frequently closed, when they are open, they track my every move. When he doesn't follow me to another room, I bribe him with a treat. It soothes me to have him always nearby: in the bedroom, my office, the porch and, yes, the bathroom where, if you must know, he works his head between my knees for me to scratch behind his ears. Other than eating and yowling when the mail arrives, this is the best part of his day and, in a way, mine too. Maybe he isn't so bored after all.

WORRIED ABOUT
MY DOG'S SELF-ESTEEM
2010

When I was a kid, I thought if only I could wear a suit of armor, I'd be safe from intruders. Then, when I learned about conductivity, I gave up the armor idea, realizing I'd have a disaster on my hands in the event of a fire.

At night, I would fall asleep clinging to my mattress, so that kidnappers would be forced to drag both me and my bed out of the house. My older sister, with whom I shared a pink room, wasn't fearful the way I was. She got the genes for green eyes and calm; I got the ones for brown eyes and worry.

These days I'm looking for a metaphorical suit of armor to keep me safe. Maybe the right kind of canine. I've heard that cows sit down when it's about to rain. I bet dogs can learn to forecast earthquakes and tsunamis. Research shows dogs can detect certain cancers on a person's breath. And, as every worrywart knows, beagles can learn to sniff for bedbugs.

I'm amazed that Casey, being a hound and all, has almost no sense of smell. After I began worrying about him being bored, we started playing this game in which I show him a kibble and act as though I'm putting it under one pillow, then I sneak it under a nearby pillow, and it takes him ages to find it without a hint. The whole time he wags his tail like crazy and afterwards I tell him he won the game even though I'm the one who won.

The same thing happens when I drop a kibble on the wooden floor, whose color blends with the treat. Casey will sniff an eighth of an inch away from his prize and then veer off toward West Virginia. Eventually he makes his way back to find it, and I say, "Wow! Good job! Good job!!"

I shower all this praise on Casey to boost his self-esteem, but is it possible he thinks he's supposed to miss the little brown kibble when I throw it? And then he thinks he's supposed to pretend to forage, looking puzzled, heightening the excitement for me, even though all the while he knows it's under the hall table?

Now that he's old, Casey sometimes sleeps through a UPS delivery; nonetheless, when he is awake, the thing he still does best is roar a terrible roar when someone steps onto the path that leads to our house. This, along with a good burglar alarm, makes me feel secure, which is not how I felt for years after I walked into the front office of my father's textile factory during an armed robbery when I was ten.

After the robbery, I had to keep the light on in my bedroom. I went to sleep clutching not only my mattress but also my autograph hound, Harry, on whose face I had drawn a smile that soothed me deep in the night. Come to think of it,

Casey's profile bears a remarkable resemblance to Harry's.

For as long as I can remember I have been worrying what it will be like when Casey dies. (To a worrywart, the here and now is overrated.) And even before Casey dies, how will I manage when he is no longer able to mount the stairs to the bedroom at the precise time my back is no longer strong enough to carry all thirty-two pounds of him?

My Casey is a big fraidy-cat and would be terrified to go in a basket with a pulley attached for me to haul him upstairs, so I am hatching a plan to put a bed for us in the family room, the way I did after my hip got replaced.

I stare at Casey and try to imagine him not there, an empty space where his body is now warming a cavity in a sofa cushion. If I were good at crying, I would weep at the mere thought of losing this partner to whom I have adapted and with whom I have grown the way Jeff and I, so different at first, adjusted to each other's rhythms.

A subset of the worrying how things will go as Casey ages has to do with what kind of dog I'll get next. What if the next hound doesn't want to go to sleep when I do at two a.m. and awaken at ten? What if he doesn't smell delicious to me, just like Casey and my babies and my high school boyfriend, Luke, of the neck that smelled like a starched shirt? What if my new pup nags to play fetch all day long?

If my next dog can sniff cancer in the early stages and detect bedbugs, I'll overlook predicting earthquakes. And if he's light enough for me to pick up as we age together, that alone will be just fine.

I worry that writing about Casey dying will jinx him. But if I allow jinxing thinking to control me, this worrywart will be left with nothing to put on the page.

So Long, Mom

MOTHER DIED TODAY
SATURDAY, JULY 2, 2011

Mother died today. I am not trying to channel Camus, just trying to make sense of how it feels to suddenly become a sixty-five-year-old orphan in New York City while my mom's cold body lies in Philadelphia. People grieve differently, so I'll try to stop worrying that my heart feels numb right now, ignorant of grief.

I'm sitting in Union Square, one of my favorite places to work when I visit New York. The usual bustle is going on around me, a pair of Boston terriers rollicking in the dog run and farmers market vendors briskly trading consumables, like the quart of organic skim milk in a glass bottle I bought to go with the slice of homemade chocolate chip banana cake I brought here in my bike basket.

A church group on a neighboring bench are painting one another's faces red, white, and blue for their annual pamphlet giveaway to promote patriotism and Christ. We take a picture together, my first thought being I can't wait to show Mom, even as I know from my brother's phone call an hour ago that, with her hand in his, my mom had taken her last breath.

I so wanted to be there with her, but one never knows when the end will happen. I knew she was in the homestretch, and though I saw her last week, I figured she would hold tight until my visit tomorrow.

It's comforting to know I spent so much quality time with Mom, yet would a better daughter, knowing her mother was rapidly failing, have rushed to her side and remained there till the end? Would it have mattered to Mom in her remote state or would that have been only for me?

A few weeks ago when I kissed her good-bye before heading home to D.C., I said, "See you next week, Mom." And she asked, "Why?"

Although a few days ago my brother reported that Mom's eyes began to be closed more often than open, I had planned to read to her, the way I had the last time I saw her. It was my fantasy that she would then slip into death, her hand in my carbon-copy, arthritic hand.

So now, who will delight in hearing what I do and what I think about every day, and who will want to see every photograph I take?

Proceeding with my planned bike ride this afternoon seems odd. At the same time, it's as though my mom died after we moved her from Florida to Philadelphia, when I realized she would never again be talking to me on the phone from her club chair, the one my dad had sat in until he died five years ago and she inherited his throne.

I can just see her. *Books, magazines and newspapers are*

stacked on the table beside her, while she watches Meet the Press *on the TV in her mirror-backed wall unit. Figurines on glass shelves reflect sunbeams. She cranks up the volume and during commercials, she surfs channels, wielding the remote with the facility of a man.*

On this day of my mother's death, I remain with my plans to meet my friend Anita at a café called Joe for a cup of joe.

I tell Anita, "My mother died this morning," and her expression of shock I am sure is greater than mine was when my phone rang this morning and I saw my brother's name appear on the display. "Mommy died," I said with certainty when I answered.

After coffee, Anita and I pedal into Brooklyn for a look at local culture and a bite of lunch.

Mom would have loved hearing about the Hasidic family I pass on the Williamsburg Bridge, the gaggle of kids following behind the father, who is wearing white tights and a long black coat that flaps as he walks. Mom would have known the Yiddish term for his big fur hat.

We stop for lunch at Fada, reported to be the only authentically French bistro in the area. Happily, there is nothing pretentious about this place, which feels as though it's been here since the invention of French fries.

We sit on high stools at a counter in the front corner, where windows are open to the street on two sides. My appetite has not faded with the loss of my mom. Rather, as I dig into my *salade Niçoise*, I recognize my anesthetized sensation to be what some friends have reported feeling after their parents died.

My mom's was a life well-lived, that ran its course with few regrets. How many of us will end up that fortunate? This doesn't minimize how much I will miss our unhurried nightly calls and our monthly weekend visits, along with her laughter, her insights, her contentedness that set the bar high—yet provided a great role model—for when I reach my walker years, if I do.

Pedaling back toward the city, I pass an African arts festival and shops shuttered for the Sabbath with names like Schenkel's Fish Market, more of the kind of travelogue Mom would have relished.

On the Manhattan Bridge, high over the East River, I feel closer to the clouds, and cheesy as it sounds, closer to Mom.

IN SEARCH OF GRIEF
2011

Grief: keen mental suffering or distress over affliction or loss; sharp sorrow; painful regret.

At the private burial, my sister and brother stand teary with their arms around each other's backs as our mother's coffin is lowered into her grave. Dry-eyed, I step up next to them to complete our sibling trio. Yet we are two plus one, a double and a single, a duet and a solo.

After standing there for several seconds, unconnected—not part of their grief, not feeling their pain—I step back to allow them their moment.

We all adored my mom and felt a closeness to her that any mother would envy.

So what's with me and this blank reaction to her death?

Like my mom, I am not a crier, except when I got divorced

and had to agree to live nine consecutive days a month without my kids. But that was years ago, and Mom was right when she told me I would come to make the most of those days on my own.

Although I can get weepy if I accidentally turn on the evening news, I strive to avoid sadness and pain. A mother's death is one of the big boppers of loss and maybe I've put up a wall to block that. Or am I just citing a psycho-notion, a result of having spent too much time in shrinks' offices?

On a similar note, maybe I am in the denial phase, though after my father died, I also wondered why I never crumbled with grief. Mom often said she wished she had been able to cry when Daddy died. Nonetheless, her heartache was palpable after sixty-six years of marriage, one in which each considered the other before themselves.

It feels counterintuitive to prance around with my life the same as I did when I had a mother, but the fact that she and I shared the dry-eyes trait pleases and reassures me. I celebrate that Mom lived ninety-two years with no misgivings, and despite my jolly demeanor, I am quite aware that her death leaves me with a permanent hollow space.

Mom was the only person in the world who thought I ought to be on *Oprah* (I'm not sure for what); Oprah, who—by ending her show—also left a void in my life. Mom timed her death nicely to coincide with the *Oprah* loss. Now, I won't have to watch an *Oprah* program about, say, octogenarian sex, and then ache to phone and discuss it with Mom.

The truth is that I lost my mom a few days after we moved her up north in a medical van to the long-term care facility (she hated the expression nursing home) near my brother's family. During the trip, Mom was her fun-loving self. She said it felt surreal, as though she were traveling to heaven, even though she didn't believe in heaven.

A few days after arriving at the nursing home, however, reality struck. Maybe her slide began on the first day when I went with her to play bingo. It was so clear how out of place she felt in a bingo game where each number had to be repeated three times. B10, pause, B10, pause, B10. No one in the room except for the woman calling the numbers looked anything like my mom, with alert eyes, upright head, and slightly rouged cheeks.

Mom's new room—where we hung her favorite paintings and arranged her personal things, like the book of drawings and tales of her life I had made for her ninetieth birthday—embodied all the railroad clichés: the final stop, the terminus, the end of the line.

She no longer wanted to live and I was her cheerleader, chanting *rah rah sis boom bah* for her to die. She reminded me how I'd always said I would help her pull the plug. "Susan, you promised," she told me. Of course when it came down to it, I could do no such thing without the approval of my siblings, the ones who know how to cry.

A few weeks after my mother became downhearted, the doctors increased her meds. Although she was still coherent, she had become non-reactive, the opposite of the mother I had always known, the mother who thrilled to everything.

Another upcoming loss is likely to be my Casey, given that he has already reached his life expectancy. Like Mom he has had a long run with few regrets, except he probably wishes I'd have taught him to fetch.

After all these years, my heart still goes pitty pat when I look at that boy. And even though he doesn't have much to say about the economy, he is great company day and night. How will I feel if he dies and I can't stop crying, considering I didn't weep when Mom died?

I'm told people grieve in their own ways, so I'll try to stop worrying that my heart isn't swollen with grief right now, right after my precious mom died.

Saving E-Mail, Saving Voice Mail
2011

I'm a saver. My three inboxes total more than fifteen thousand e-mails. Who knows, someday I may want to check out correspondence from Sock Hop Sundays, Hot Tub Works or Book TV. Plus, I don't want to waste time deleting or unsubscribing.

Aside from highlighting my hedonistic tendencies, these e-mails reveal the fear I'll miss something, even though I have never opened a Book TV alert and I attended a Sock Hop Sunday only once. With phone messages, it's different. I so fear accumulating my kids' voices, far more precious than e-mail, that I delete them right away so as not to tempt any hoarding demons.

Five months after my mother died, I was visiting Eliza in New York when, in preparation for trading her Blackberry for an iPhone, she was transferring to her computer twenty voice messages she had saved. Except for the few times Eliza made me hold my ears, I listened. I heard the message from me singing "Happy Birthday." And then the room filled with the voice most familiar of all.

"Lizie, it's Grandmom. The book you sent me, I never laughed so much! (laughter) I laughed out loud the whole time I was reading it. (laughter) I just loved it . . . It was so funny! (more laughter)"

Before my mom became ill, Eliza had asked me to take *Shopoholic* to her in Florida. "I think Grandmom will like it," she'd said. My mom died a few months later. On Christmas Day Mom would have been ninety-three, the birth date she shared with Eliza.

Hearing my mother's voice and that laugh—so real, so hearty, so alive—was like having her right there on the sofa with Eliza and me, making me feel so happy, so sad.

Now that I have this recording of my mom's voice to treasure, I'm wondering whether I should start saving the voice mail messages from everyone I love as well as a recording of Casey's bark. Oy.

SEARCHING FOR
SUSAN FISHMAN

BOYFRIENDS AGAIN
1997 - 1998

For several months after the separation, each time the kids went to Jeff, I boarded a train to New York, where I stayed with my friends Joan and Richard and their daughter, Rebecca, who was born three days after Eliza. Joan listened to my troubles as she prepared warm chicken dinners. She counseled me deep into the nights, while Richard, a humor writer, interjected wisecracks, sometimes directed at Jeff, an easy target, who did things like produce the only anniversary present he'd given me in a decade two weeks after we separated. Rebecca assumed the role of caring fourth child who never talked back. My morning walks in their Upper East Side neighborhood were the hard part. From every direction, converging toward me—as though flaunting—mothers walked hand-in-hand with their children en route to school, which was how my world ought to have been.

My identity as my daughters' nurturer was so deep in my core that I could not fathom recovering entirely from the anguish of not being there to take them to every birthday party, every orthodontist appointment. The loss felt like something between an amputation and a death. On these New York outings, I talked and talked while friends listened. I listened to their tales of hardship too, which admittedly comforted me.

Late one night on C-Span I heard Isabel Allende speak about the ability of the human spirit to rise above adversity, and my outlook began to brighten. After all, her daughter had died. My eyes began to dry and my chatter became sprinkled with boy talk; soon it became mostly boy talk. Everyone offered advice: "When you go to the supermarket, groom like it's opening night at the opera. You never know who you'll bump into." "Play hard to get." "Volunteer at a hospice, so you can meet men whose wives are dying."

In New York and without my girls, I had the time and mental space to contemplate how—as a newly single woman—I fit into the universe. And unlike in Washington, in Manhattan I was always squished up against people. I could have mute interactions and imaginary conversations. One afternoon I saw a man eating in an Upper East Side coffee shop, and I had this urge to walk in, sit down opposite him, lean forward, and ask, "What's your impression of me? I'm newly separated. Do you think anyone will want to date me?"

Another time, near Grand Central Station, I asked an impeccably tailored man if he knew where I could find a watch repair shop. He had the most hypnotizing blue eyes. After he disappeared in the lunchtime crowd, I envisioned an invention of a headband with antennae and little colored bulbs that people could wear and operate with a remote control to emit silent signals of interest by bending an antenna in someone's direction and flashing a blinking green light. Sometimes I think about that man's eyes, and I picture him at the dinner table in Scarsdale with his wife in her burgundy jogging suit and their bright, athletic, blue-eyed kids.

Then there were times, usually when Jeff was picking on me for something like taking the children on a vacation during a week that he was available to see them, that I walked down the street muttering in my head at every man I passed, *You're a snake. And you're a snake. You're all snakes.* Women were so much easier to deal with. I wished I could will myself to become a lesbian.

I was bothered by the superficiality of all this worry about meeting men. Many women I knew had no desire to date, and their lives were far more productive than mine. Since I was not inclined to shut down my interest, I opened my mind to expand the universe of possibilities. I readdressed all the notions I'd formed in my teens and twenties about the opposite sex, so that now I could consider someone a prospect even if he were wearing, say, his jeans hiked up too high.

Looking up unattached guys from my past seemed like a good idea. Brian and I had never dated, though we had once kissed in a taxi. He was the close friend of a former boyfriend of mine; I had met both of them on a ski vacation half my life ago. When Brian heard my voice on the phone, he sounded cheered. I told him I was in New York, and he said I should come see him.

I arrived at the same rent-controlled building in the East Eighties that Brian had lived in for as long as I'd known him. On the elevator, I tried to conjure up a picture of him. Although his nose was too prominent and his lips too thin,

I had always hovered on the edge of being attracted to him. I liked his slender build, the navy sweater and corduroys he always wore, and his easy laughter. When he opened the door, my eyes landed on his thick, silver and black hair. A lot of hair was something Jeff wished he had. As revenge, I plotted to find a boyfriend with no bare spots on his scalp.

Brian gave me a big hug and led me to a small Formica table in his kitchenette, where I sat while he sliced a couple of bagels and brewed two cups of coffee. While he told me how he had cried for months after his marriage had ended years earlier and about single life, the minute hand on his kitchen clock made three quick revolutions. He spoke about the last person he had gone out with. "I slept with her on the third date, then I never saw her again." I tried to reconcile his treatment of women with his soft side that had given up investment banking to work with needy children. The way he avoided commitment made me wonder what was in store for me, with him or some other bachelor.

Seizing this as a research opportunity, I asked, "What do you think of women who get a little nip and tuck?" I placed my fingers on my jaws and stretched the skin toward my ears.

"I think it's fine. I would do it myself," he replied.

I was disappointed that he did not instead say, "Oh, you look great. You don't have to worry about that." Then I looked closely at his eyes and wondered whether his face had already experienced an encounter with a scalpel. Ick.

He walked me outside where a light mist tickled my face. As I looked up at him to say good-bye, I wrapped my new chenille scarf of autumn colors twice around my neck and felt attractive for the first time since my separation.

He put his arms around me and said, "Let me know when you're coming back to New York."

The following month, my visit with Brian began much as it had the first time, except this time we sat in his living room, I on the couch with my feet on the coffee table and he on a large, worn, Archie Bunker chair with his arms folded across his chest. Picking up on our previous conversation about single life in the nineties, he told me I was hanging out at all the right places—Starbucks, gym, bookstores—and offered the information he had previously hinted at, that sex usually occurred on the third or fourth date. "The girl is in charge of condoms," he said. I wondered whether this counted as our second date.

We went out to a dessert cafe, where we sat at a tiny table beside a window adorned with white Christmas lights and ordered chocolate gelato—one dish, two spoons. Afterwards, Brian once again opened his arms wide and embraced me, not letting go for minutes, kissing my cheek while layers of coats separated us.

On my walk back to Joan's, I savored the memory of the evening. Soon, though, the analysis began. *Pretty intimate good-bye for an old buddy. I wonder whether he likes me. He paid for the ice cream. But how come he didn't ask me back to his place? Afraid? Looking out for me? Sparing an old friend the aggravation of falling for him (too late for that perhaps)? Had I missed a cue to turn my mouth to his?*

The following day on the Metroliner back to Washington, I felt all dreamy, swilling a Samuel Adams out of the bottle and listening to my Johnny Mathis audiotape, *Sixteen Greatest Hits.* The Johnny Mathis thing was my innermost se-

cret, my *Penthouse Forum*, my peek-a-boo lingerie, my Porn.
com, my leather and chains. My independent, tough-guy side
viewed this proclivity for cornball sound as an embarrassing
sexual deviation. In the privacy and anonymity of my train
seat, where the other passengers might as well have been crash
dummies, it was safe to indulge in romantic fantasy while Johnny crooned, "I'll love you till the poets run out of rhyme . . ."
Like no one else could, Johnny Mathis carried me back to
memories of making out in boys' parents' bedrooms and to the
fluttery sensations of high school. Only now, rather than the
chipped-toothed smile of Luke, the face in my mental filmstrip
belonged to Brian in his Yankees cap, and there I am, living in
that little apartment with him, jointly parenting our adopted
baby boy, the natural progression from hugging in coats.

My weakness for love songs was satisfied during the early stages with Jeff. Setting up the record player, which always
included his favorite album by The Carpenters, was part of a
ritual that also included candles and wine. When did the acces-
sories of lovemaking disappear? When was the last time we'd
had a make-out kiss that was not part of making love? I used
to wonder whether, if we had really paid attention and agreed
to have one of those big mouth kisses every day, it would have
been enough to fan the passion. If I had no one to dream about,
that gooey music got on my nerves; I needed to connect it to
someone who gave me goose bumps. Jeff, on the other hand,
never tired of the light FM sound. Without my fully realizing it
at the time, the more Jeff and I grew apart, the more irritated I
became when I had to listen to Karen Carpenter.

I called Brian two weeks in advance to let him know I
would be back in New York. As he had the previous month,
he suggested I come to his apartment on a Saturday evening.

Then, the Tuesday before our date, he left a message at nine forty-two a.m. on my answering machine for me to call him. My whole body slumped, because the only reason he would be calling on a weekday morning was to break the date. I reached him at two that afternoon.

"Hi," he said, and then paused before continuing. "Uh, I was wondering what you think about the idea of us having," he paused again, "a sexual relationship."

This was why he had phoned? There was something about the question popping up on a weekday morning that made it seem especially implausible.

"Is this how it's done in the nineties?" I asked, feeling giggly inside. He suggested I come, earlyish. Although I was flattered, I wondered whether he was a little zany, making an appointment for a first sexual encounter. I was not ready to have sex with him, but I thought about it all week.

Before leaving Joan and Richard's that Saturday night, in the event I were to stay at Brian's until the following day, I rumpled my bed so it would look like I had slept there, just in case Rebecca were to pass my room in the morning. This role reversal did not escape me: I, the grown-up, was sneaking around, worrying that Rebecca, the eighteen-year-old, would find out. Considering how much as a teenager I had to sneak around, it distressed me to think that, with three daughters plus Rebecca, there would be no end to my sneaking, complete freedom forever beyond my reach.

When I arrived at Brian's nearly an hour later than he had expected, he seemed annoyed. Although I suffered from habitual lateness, I could have done better. The reason my mental clock was so far off probably had to do with some need I had for the upper hand, a calculated indifference that boosted my confidence. Even though I had not consciously scheduled myself to be nearly an hour late, I had done nothing to accelerate my pace, which included a lengthy visit with a friend and her house guest, a handsome divorced man up from Florida. I interpreted Brian's displeasure to mean he cared. My desire to get a rise out of him proved that my dating IQ had not advanced in thirty years.

Brian had made plans to meet friends for dinner, so there was no time for our usual chat. The meal seemed to take forever, heightening the sexual tension. After we bid his friends farewell, we walked back to his apartment, where I sat exactly as I had the previous month, in the middle of the sofa with my feet up, assuming he would take his place beside me. Instead, he sank into his armchair, hugging himself as before. Our talking, too, picked up where we had left it, as if for the past thirty one days we had been bolted into place, droning on about being single, devising tactics to find someone, yet avoiding commitment. When I asked what inspired his phone call on Tuesday, the spiral toward resolution seemed to begin at last.

"It was just a spontaneous, fun idea I woke up with that day," he said.

Spontaneous? How spontaneous did he expect it to be if I had time to consult my psychiatrist and my lawyer? I told him that, aside from it being a little soon in our relationship (my psychiatrist's contribution), Jeff and I had not yet signed a separation agreement (my lawyer's contribution). I wondered how long Brian and I would continue this verbal waltz and how I could achieve my goal of making out without going past first base.

Finally it occurred to me to ask, "Does it have to be all or nothing?"

"No," he answered.

"Well in that case…," I said, allowing my words to trail off, which was when he came over and sat beside me.

He asked, "Would it be okay for me to kiss you?" I nodded, and he did.

I did not remember all this asking from my previous round of single years, although it would have made dating much more bearable if guys I had gone out with had requested permission before forcing their lips on my face at the door. It would have avoided a lot of strategic planning to escape contact at the end of a date. I figured Brian's questions were his way of avoiding rejection, which surprised me, because he had been at this for decades and he seemed so self-assured. I wondered whether I brought out his insecurities. I hoped so.

Being too much of a hedonist to cut short something that felt as good as snuggling close to Brian, I made no move to go home. I had a lot of feeling good to catch up on after so many months of feeling lousy.

Brian did not force himself on me, which aroused memories of those deliciously frustrating sessions on dead end streets in Luke's father's Porsche, wanting more but adhering to my "standards." I had standards now too, although I had not figured out what they were. For sure, the risk of contracting sexually transmitted diseases was a big obstacle for someone like me who avoided touching escalator handrails and who considered double dipping to be chancy. My reservations also stemmed from my self-image as a mother, which included a belief that I ought to conduct myself the way I wanted my daughters to conduct themselves. Moreover, I remembered that my richest relationships had advanced gradually.

Brian led me to the bedroom and threw a flannel shirt to me. I changed in the bathroom, after which we rolled around for a while and then lay still. As Brian's breathing became deep with slumber, memories of long-ago boyfriends seeped into my mind along with flashbacks to horny, sleepless nights in big, borrowed flannel shirts. Brian's covers weighed less than I required for a sound sleep in the best of circumstances. Yet I dared not move, because earlier he had shown me his new vitamin shipment, which was his latest attempt to cure his insomnia.

The morning was worth the long wait. Brian regaled me with tales about the cranky man in the dirty coffee shop on Second Avenue that had the best bagels in all of New York. Drawing the conversation back to our favorite topic, I asked whether he had ever had phone sex, thinking, but not saying, that although I never had, it might be an option for us in the future. He told me he had once called a nine hundred number and a girl talked dirty while he masturbated. "You know," I said, "they can figure out who you are with Caller ID."

"Oh God," he replied, with a look of wide-eyed, wide-mouthed horror. "I'll never do that again."

Ready to wash up, I admitted I'd stuck a toothbrush in my bag—just in case. When I opened the medicine cabinet to set my wet toothbrush on a shelf, an array of grooming products stared out at me, many with dirt in the grooves of their caps. They fascinated me by their variety and sheer numbers, yet I never wanted to picture a guy using anything besides deodorant, shaving cream, shampoo, and toothpaste.

I wished I had not noticed there was no soap on the sink. Clearly, I had taken this in the night before, but I must have already reached my mental capacity with everything else that was going on. Holding a tissue over the knob, I opened the door and tried to banish the no-soap from my thoughts.

I found Brian in the kitchen grinding coffee beans. When

I entered, the whirring stopped. I put my arms around him from behind and he turned and kissed me. In the light that streamed in through a small window, I was aware of being more attracted to his mind and body than to his face. It helped that I was eye-level with his chin. As with the no-soap, I quickly dismissed anything about his looks that detracted from my interest; I wanted to be gaga over him.

We slipped into our jackets and then headed out to buy the acclaimed bagels. Walking along Second Avenue with Brian— as good as it felt—seemed strange, same as it always had after crossing the border from friendship with a guy to something more amorous. Without the protective walls of his apartment and boundaries of his couch, kitchenette chairs, and bed, and without enough time before us to chew on analyses of why relationships fail, my brain did its usual blackout.

A big subject, such as what went wrong in Brian's marriage, risked getting chopped up with interruptions from the bagel man. Yet silence felt awkward. Years earlier, at a yard sale, I had bought a book by Barbara Walters, *How to Talk with Practically Anyone about Practically Anything*, which I kept on a shelf in my bedroom and referred to from time to time, but regardless of how much research I did, the more I cared about finding something to say, the more I could expect words to escape me. Even the lists I had compiled decades earlier of topics to talk about, in case a guy I liked phoned, made for staccato conversation; they threw off my timing; I recalled moving to a new topic, aborting a satisfying conclusion to the previous subject, or skipping, without transition, from, say, why I thought there should be bike lanes in city streets to why I was weaning myself from caffeine. Did this happen to everyone or just me?

I wondered why Brian was not saying much either. Did

he like me so much that words had escaped him too? Where had I acquired the notion that silence was worse than chatter? Maybe my silences were caused by a shyness I was not aware I had? Was shyness always bad or were there people who like being shy? Was my need to fill conversation gaps a Jewish thing? In restaurants, I rarely saw quiet Jews.

While Brian was waiting for our bagels to be "schmeared" I told him, "I'll be right back." Without listening for a response, I ran outside and rounded the corner into a small grocery store to buy liquid hand cleanser. As soon as we returned to his apartment, I placed the soap on the rim of his bathroom sink.

Settled into breakfast with each of us burrowed into a section of the newspaper, I marveled at my good fortune: waking up on a Sunday morning in New York beside a man I liked, and then feasting on bagels, coffee, and *The New York Times* in his one-bedroom apartment.

As if that were not enough, it also happened to be the day the Monica Lewinsky story broke. So now I had the guy, the bagels, the coffee, *The Times*, and a political sex scandal. I told myself that whatever happened, even if I never had another date in my whole life, I would have this memory to carry to the nursing home and cherish while rocking beside a ruffle-curtained window.

We watched a dozen repetitions of Monica getting her presidential hug. Brian predicted Clinton would be impeached. I interpreted this conjecture to be less a thoughtful analysis of the President's predicament than a reflection of Brian's Republican leanings, which troubled me, but not that much because I figured at some point I could talk him out of being a Republican, the way I had always anticipated calling upon my communication skills to convince a rapist not to assault me.

At five p.m., wanting to stay the longest possible amount of time, but with me being the first to suggest I leave—*The Price is Right* of departures—I said I had things to do. He said, "Me too." As I stood waiting for the elevator, Brian watched from his doorway and then waved good-bye.

Around now I ought to acknowledge that my instincts for balancing Brian's need for space with my need for intimacy were all wrong. The next day I phoned him to say I was heading back to D.C. the following morning and to suggest we get together, because otherwise we would not see each other for three weeks. He said he had too much work to do.

Brian's resistance made me wonder about my role in the demise of our mini-relationship. How could I have missed that our little PJ party was not sufficient justification for me to drop anchor in his quarters two days during the same week? I had this strong suspicion, which turned out to be accurate, that I was never going to see my toothbrush again.

BLUE JACKET
1997

A t times during that first year after my separation it seemed my filters were entirely absent. On New Year's Eve, I was shopping at my neighborhood gourmet market, and beside me at the cheese counter stood this fair-haired, thirty-ish man in a bright blue ski jacket. It was not just that he was so boyishly good-looking, in that smooth, hairless way one imagines appeals to a pedophilic priest. Without exchanging a word, noticing how his face lit up I wanted to bask in his glow. That's how monstrously scrambled my brain was.

I figured the cheese man knew him, because I heard them talking about a mutual acquaintance. After Blue Jacket walked away, I said to the cheese man, "He's cute. Do you think he could ever be interested in an older woman?"

The cheese man replied, "He moved up here from Atlanta to be with a woman who's older than he is, but I'm not sure they're still together. I'll ask him when he comes back to pick up his order."

"Okay," I said, "I'll check with you in a little while." I proceeded to fill my basket with nuts, pâtés, and chocolates for the hundred and twenty guests my children and I were expecting at our open house eighteen hours later. Not wanting to appear over-anxious, I allowed more than sufficient time before revisiting the cheese man.

"I'm sorry. I forgot to ask him," he said.

Downhearted, I wheeled my cart toward the registers in the back of the store. To my joy, there was Blue Jacket in line with one customer behind him. Instinctively, I headed to the adjacent line. My mind was jumping all over the place, my heart pitter-pattering. What could I say to him? Before I could come up with a scheme, he was pocketing his change and moving through the automatic door. My opportunity was about to vanish into the darkness, forever. So I abandoned my basket and ran out after him.

"Excuse me," I said. "I just wanted to ask, are you attached to anyone and, if not, am I too old for you?" He smiled and shone his luminous eyes down on me, "I'm flattered. Actually, I am seeing someone. But if I weren't, you wouldn't be too old."

I smiled back and said, "Well, Happy New Year, anyway."

"Happy New Year to you too," he answered.

An hour later, I put on shorts, a T-shirt, knee and wrist guards, slung roller blades over my shoulder, and plugged a Walkman into my ears for my friends' California-themed New Year's Eve party, all the while visualizing Blue Jacket balancing his groceries on his thigh as he opened the door to his hungry Joan Crawford in her feathery high-heeled slippers, the two of them then stretching out on a zebra rug and popping Gorgonzola into each other's mouths before a crackling fire.

I tried to rewrite the script. What if he had been available? We could have had our first kiss at midnight. He would have met my children and everyone we knew at our open house. Had I appeared to be propositioning him? I had not intended to forsake my post-divorce virginity that night, but only to communicate that I would like to have a date with him. It was hard to know what was expected in male-female encounters and harder yet to figure out what I expected of myself.

A few days later, when I related the encounter to my psychiatrist, he asked, "This really happened or you just imagined it?"

Clearly he believed that what I did was so outlandish, it must have occurred only in my imagination. That, of all people, my therapist seemed startled by my escapade made me wonder whether I was teetering on a ledge atop a flaming skyscraper.

Nonetheless, for the rest of the winter, I kept an eye out for that blue jacket.

CONFESSIONS OF AN
IDENTITY THIEF
1998

Growing up, I associated my last name, Fishman, with the smell of pickled herring that clung to my grandfather's mustache on Sunday mornings. In college, friends called me Fish, which I accepted as an expression of endearment.

When I married Jeff and revised the name on my library card to match my husband's, friends equated that with forsaking my individuality. Yet I was secretly pleased to be shedding my original name's cat-food image. What I had not anticipated was the dilemma I would eventually face when phoning editors, who would assume I was Susan Orlean, *The New Yorker* staff writer and author of many books, including *The Orchid Thief* on which the film *Adaptation* was based.

Sixteen years into my life as Susan Orlins, I moved from New York to Washington, D.C. Although from time to time my personal essays appeared in print, they were not likely to be a topic of conversation at the water cooler. So when I dialed a *Washington Post* editor to pitch an idea and his voice mail clicked on, I thought, *There's no way this guy who never heard of me will phone back.* Yet minutes later, he returned the call. "We generally don't run first-person pieces, but I'd love to consider your manuscript. Oh, and let me give you my direct line." Then he said, "I thought you lived in Manhattan." How did he know I used to live in New York? For a moment vanity kicked in. Perhaps he remembered the op-ed piece I had penned for *Newsday* years earlier or one of my articles from deep in the business section of *The Sunday New York Times.*

Then he said, "That's Susan OrLEAN?"

"Orlins," I confessed. "O-r-l-i-n-s." In the silence that followed, his disappointment was palpable. I began to notice that other editors returned my calls promptly, often promising to respond to submissions within a day or two, rather than the usual six months. One woman, on her way to the airport, recited her itinerary and said, "I'll get back to you the second I return."

I confronted an ethical quandary. Just because an editor gave me his fax number, was I to assume it was a case of mistaken identity? Because someone listed on a masthead was not rude to me, did I have to tell who I was not? What if my birth certificate happened to have said Barbara Walters? Would it have been wrong to leverage what was rightfully mine when making dinner reservations at restaurants where desirable tables went only to patrons whose smiles had graced the pages of *Vanity Fair*? Or, if a voice on the phone had twittered, "Oh-la-la, Ms. Walters," would the correct response have been, "I am not who you think I am, so it's okay to seat me next to the men's room"?

Up to this point I'd had no hand in chicanery. Yet I found myself stalked by a notion that my acceptance rate would soar if I were to extend the illusion to editors that I was Susan

Orlean; I rationalized that I could compose an essay about the experience, the way some journalists feign homelessness for the sake of a firsthand story.

I began with my byline, deleting Fishman, which I used only to make an impression on high school classmates who might have stumbled upon my writing. And when leaving messages, instead of saying "My name is Susan Orlins," I said, "This is Susan Orlins," which sounded more like an assumption the callee ought to have known who I was.

These manipulations may not seem like a big deal, but I am not a fibber. In fact, one could argue that I am a compulsive truth-teller, the type who leaves a note after sideswiping a parked car. So the slim possibility that I was leading people on felt as though I had masterminded a full-blown cover up. Plus, I was terrified of getting caught, which probably accounted for my whole history of post-teenage scrupulousness.

Although I told myself I had simply let slip a couple of the two hundred falsehoods the average citizen supposedly commits each day, shame haunted me. I started to believe I was an impostor even to call myself a writer, and that I had chosen to become a personal essayist in the first place because it enabled me to misrepresent my life through crafty editing—more flimflam.

It was time to reform. When an editor at *Washingtonian* said she would gladly look at a piece I pitched, I told her, "I'm not who you think I am. I'm Susan Orlins, not Susan Orlean"

"Who's Susan Orlean?" she asked. Go figure.

The following week I was getting my hair cut at Robert Stuart in New York. Now, the reason I went to this Upper West Side salon was because I had read a *New Yorker* article—written by Susan Orlean—about its chatty ambiance. I should also tell you that when I had seen Susan's chronicle, I thought, "Why didn't I think to write about beauty parlor culture?" It was difficult not to read competitively.

"That's Susan Orlean," whispered Robert, pausing from feathering my bangs and from his monologue about why he wanted me to use a rinse to eliminate my bits of gray. A trench-coated woman, whose strawberry hair swung jauntily about her face and shoulders, whizzed behind my freshly cropped reflection.

She was one of those people who arrive at the hairdresser looking better than those leaving. At least that is how I remember her. Perhaps Robert pointed her out because whenever I called for an appointment, it created confusion as to which Susan I was. Surely he did not suspect the truth—that I had brushed away as too unlikely reveries that I might actually bump into her.

Susan emerged from the dressing room just after Robert finished blowing the loose hairs off my neck. The identical taupe wraps she and I wore had an equalizing effect.

"Hi," I said to her. "My name is Susan Orlins. I'm also a writer and whenever I phone editors, they fawn all over me, thinking I'm you."

"Tell me more," she said. "No one fawns all over me." I recounted two fawnings from the previous month. The conversation meandered to children; I had three and she had none, yet I rattled on about the advantages of certain nursery schools in the city versus others. I liked that I knew more about something than she did.

Afterward, peering at my new hairdo in the reflection of a shop window, I mused that I ought to have given Susan my phone number in case someday an editor were to call her thinking she was Susan Orlins.

WHEN MY FRIEND DIED
2004

Some worrywarts—me for example—dwell on the past, which can manifest as regret. I rarely saw my old friend Lou, other than at my annual New Year's Day open house. Then he died and I thought *Why didn't I talk to him more at my party?* I immediately wanted to go to lunch with him. The logical thought that followed was *Who might die next?* This kind of thinking could lead to a lot of unnecessary lunches.

SWINGIN' SATURDAY NIGHT
2005

It's Saturday night and I'm steppin' out. In the full-length mirror on my closet door, I glance with approval as I twirl and my polka-dot skirt flares. I knot a small, silk scarf above the neckline of my pink short-sleeved sweater. While slipping into my wedge-heeled dancing shoes, whose suede soles are smooth as rose petals, I pop two peppermint Chiclets into my mouth, and then I am off to the weekly swing dance in the Spanish Ballroom at Glen Echo, a former amusement park.

Driving along the winding, moonlit road, I enter a zone of mystery even though, having made this excursion dozens of times since my divorce, I know what to expect: I'll Lindy Hop the way I did in my high school gym, but instead of "Runaround Sue" on a forty-five, there will be the big trumpet sound of a live band. Young women wearing pancake makeup and Judy Garland pageboys, rolled under hairnets fine as spider webs, will attract the most nimble-footed men.

Except for The Cowboy—he'll save a dance for me. If you go to Glen Echo on a Saturday night, you will recognize The Cowboy in his Texas boots that make a clopping sound whenever he stomps on the scuffed maple floor. Like everyone at the swing dance he is nameless to me, but I'll bet he has a story.

By the time I enter the crowded parking lot, I have slipped fully into character: from an over-involved mother, who grew up jitterbugging in Philly, into a gal, named Dot perhaps, from a small Midwestern town, with hardly a care at this moment except that she will get to Lindy.

I park and stuff my purse under the driver's seat, and then walk briskly down a dark, gravel path, as though someone is chasing me, till carousel lights and a neon sign that says "OPCORN" come into view. Just before the old Cuddle Up ride—on which I cuddled up thirty-five years ago with a Paul Newman lookalike law student—the Spanish Ballroom beckons. My usual premonition that a beguiling newcomer will ask me to dance makes me feel tingly, while my jitters about facing a roomful of strangers make my breathing quicken, just enough to inspire me, the way a bit of stage fright enhances an actor's performance.

Crossing the threshold, I enter a bygone era when people dressed up to dance, and I am back in my twenties, less than half my actual age. I hand a crumpled twenty-dollar bill to a young man accessorized in two-tone beige wing tips and a newsboy cap. As proof that I have paid, he secures a neon green band around my wrist, sealing my identity as Dot. It is a mild evening, so this 1933 ballroom, where you shiver in winter and sweat like crazy in summer, feels comfortable. The lighting, yellow, as though from the passage of time, is neither bright nor dim but sufficient to see that hundreds of dancers have already formed two concentric circles, gents on the outside, ladies inside. In the center, instructors Tom and Debra are demonstrating triple step, triple step, rock step. Tom has just asked the guys to move to the right and try it with their new partners. During the one-hour lesson I will bop a few steps with fifty or so males, some older than my father, others younger than my teenage daughters.

Squinting, I search for The Cowboy, though he never shows up till after the lesson ends and the band gets going. Given the absence of an ideal spot in the circle, one where a guy with a twinkle in his eye is not too far down the line, I head for the nearest opening. I am not likely to meet my next husband in this lineup; the few appealing men always seem to be beaming at their dates across the way. But I am not here to find a mate (not that it couldn't happen). Nor am I here to learn triple step, considering the substantial portion of my developmental years that I spent jitterbugging with my bedroom doorknob and the Venetian blinds cord. I am here because I always go home feeling cheerier than when I came.

These faded walls embrace my secret world, where terrorist attacks are as remote as Jupiter and the boundaries that define my life outside the ballroom doors evaporate. None of the Fruit Fly Dads, who sell Florida grapefruits to raise money for my kids' school, show up on the dance floor, just as no swing dancers appear at my daughters' soccer games. This community, diverse as the Immigration and Naturalization Service waiting area, also provides relief from the lawn-obsessed neighborhood where I live.

But it is not merely my child-centered existence and the perfectly-trimmed-hedge mentality from which I find respite. Despite my bravado about not needing a guy (you may have already detected a note of ambivalence), having a dance hall at my disposal spares me from hanging out in the self-help aisle at Barnes & Noble on a Saturday night, exchanging glances with men who peruse corporate scandal bestsellers while their wives wait in the checkout line.

Tom and Debra do a final demonstration. Wearing wide-legged trousers, Debra—mute and loose-limbed with fidgety feet in supple black shoes that barely brush the floor—conjures an image of Charlie Chaplin. My new partner, concentrating hard to get it right, says, "I can tell you've done this before." I half-smile and nod.

This is probably a good time to admit that, while I can jitterbug and cha-cha as surely as I can walk, I struggle to maintain a beat unless my partner and I are glued hand-to-hand (which is not to say I favor serial hand-holding and the resulting germ exchange; towelettes in my glove compartment, for sanitizing my palms before I head home, attest to that).

Back in the sixties, when it became all the rage for dancing pairs to unhinge and go it alone, I found myself in a freefall of self-consciousness, just when everyone else seemed liberated. How I envy my college buddy Al, who at weddings and bar mitzvahs still does the monkey, during which he exhibits a level of public exhilaration that I can only imagine. When under pressure to join a crowd of disco dancers (is it still called disco dancing?), I go for blending in with minimal foot action and the occasional finger snap, hoping no one will notice when I fall out of step. So it should come as no surprise that my small measure of dancing success at Glen Echo, in itself, gives me reason enough to be here.

At last the O'Tones join their horns on stage and raise them to their lips, filling the air with the boogie-woogie beat of "In the Mood." A burly guy slides up to me as though I am home plate and offers his hand. "Care to dance?"

"Love to," I respond as eagerly as if he is Harrison Ford and has asked me to fly to Aspen. Don't get me wrong. My response to Burly is completely sincere. Being asked to dance—some measure of assurance that I am desirable no matter how slim the context—is another compelling reason to be here. In fact, it is entirely possible that my fulfillment from this inferred flattery exceeds the pleasure of actually dancing.

Burly does not smile; I can tell this from my peripheral vision, since I cannot deal with the intimacy of actually looking at him. My skirt swishes as I swivel this way and that, showing off with a subtle kick mid-rock step that I learned from my sister a lifetime ago. Suspending disbelief, I imagine guys on the sidelines pegging me to be their next partner. At every twirl my eyes sweep the room, straining for a glimpse of The Cowboy's silver pate. Nearby, two men are practicing triple step; beyond them, a girl in a wheelchair, wearing spotless red and white saddle shoes, swivels gaily under her partner's arm. I recognize four guys I've danced with, including one in tan suspenders who moves like an *American Bandstand* contest winner but whom I shall avoid because he smells like a decomposing mouse. This sensory business is the hard part. Bobbing up and down with a stranger whose hands are slippery with sweat is one thing, but when someone's breath is stale, well, it is hardly manageable to jump around while holding my own peppermint gum-scented breath.

I wonder whether the men who come here alone have only beer and partially-eaten sandwiches in their fridges. And where would you find these guys at, say, two-thirty on a Wednesday afternoon? Would The Cowboy be sporting a three-piece suit and cufflinks, swinging his briefcase along the avenue after a prolonged lunch with a jasmine-scented client? I doubt anyone cares that I have been at various times a street artist and a stockbroker, and that I was once on unemployment but I now own upholstered garden furniture. Is anyone besides me curious what these folks' living rooms look like at Christmastime? The only question I ever get asked is: Do you swing Hollywood-style or Savoy?

"In the Mood" ends and I nod appreciation to Burly as I back toward the ring of onlookers, a signal we will not have another go. Once, a slender guy with soulful eyes asked me to dance, and when the music stopped, I just hung beside him with excited anticipation. I pictured the usual: growing old together, broiling fish, playing Scrabble. It was the only real conversation I ever had at a swing dance, lasting long enough for me to tell him about Eliza getting suspended for her last day of high school because she got into a fist fight with a boy who threw a water balloon at her; in return, Slender Guy shared that his wife was dead, his daughter was seventeen and pregnant, and his son had recently joined AA. I placed a brick onto the "stay single" side of my imaginary balancing scale and excused myself.

Nearby a boy with skin the color of cinnamon swabs his brow with a terrycloth wristband, so I know he is not just a spectator. "Dance?" I ask. Silently he places a splayed hand on my back and guides me to an opening on the crowded floor. He has not rejected me, further evidence that on these Saturday night dates with myself the only person likely to be judging me is me. Beginning with "Double time!" he shouts a string of instructions whose meanings I can only guess. "Pretzel!" "Starburst!" "Hiphugger!" Throughout the entire number

I remain a beat behind. Mercifully the music ends. He compliments me for keeping up. It is not my fantasy, but I am curious what kind of buffet this guy offers up during sex. "Another go?" he asks and I say, "Sure, but I have to take it a little easy because I've just recovered from a hip injury." He promises no aerials and then resumes double time.

I have learned firsthand that I possess neither the stamina nor skill to keep up with another sprinter, the guy whose T-shirt says "I Thought I Was Leading." On my maiden visit to the Spanish Ballroom, I asked him to dance. This was before my enlightenment that it was overstepping, so to speak, to approach one so superior to myself. I simply thought he was dashing, his shiny black hair slicked back, same as the South Philly boys who jitterbugged under the watchful eye of Dick Clark fifty years ago. After trying a few fancy moves, he must have realized I could benefit from some lessons because he jimmied down the choreography. Subsequently, I noticed he chose his partners from the in-crowd of young ruby-lipped women who knew how to jam at breakneck speed with style and attitude.

If I really had been Dot's age, I would have yearned to fit in. Instead, peeking out from behind my Dot masquerade, the sensible, middle-aged me shoots for the more attainable. Narrowing the range of partners to my ideal one, I choose The Cowboy. I spot him in a far corner, doing the shag with a fortyish redhead, who looks dazzling in a turquoise dress.

Rather than coyly waiting for The Cowboy to find me, I work my way over to dance near him with a guy who wears a knitted cap pulled down to his eyebrows, like someone about to break into a second-story window. When Cowboy and Reds part, I sidle up and tap his shoulder. I place my hand on his open palm and he puts his other arm around my waist. The music intensifies and we move as mirror images. Then he pulls me close to his side and ever so smoothly leads me into the Charleston, which bears little resemblance to the eye-tricking, knee-swapping drill my father taught me when he was way younger than I am now. The Cowboy slows, then quickens the pace, then teases with an unexpected pause. I concentrate hard as I watch his feet, trying to predict what he'll do next, hoping my open-toed wedgies will remain not more than a nanobeat behind his pointy-toed boots.

When I mess up, I raise my head and we graze glances. We smile, he with an expression of affectionate forgiveness, which feels momentarily intimate, and I with a blush. For now, my cravings for variety and surprise are satisfied, and I know that all of tonight's dances before The Cowboy have been foreplay, some guys repeating the monotonous triple step, triple step, rock step till the music mercifully stopped. I think you can tell a thing or two about the kind of lover someone would be, not from how well he dances but by how imaginatively he moves—with nuance and the unexpected.

Always after three numbers Cowboy says, "Save me a dance before you go." Always I say yes but never do. You see, it's not like I am dying to have a sleepover with The Cowboy; rather, I am dying to keep everything precisely as it is, and three dances are just enough to suit me without the risk of spinning a sweet memory into anything but the occasional daydream and without the risk of experiencing letdown from overexposure. I take a final lap around the ballroom's perimeter to make certain I have not overlooked an opportunity.

Orange flyers announcing next week's "Bop 'n Bowl" at a duckpin alley are stacked on a table near the door. I make a mental note to go. I aim a friendly nod at Beige Wing Tips who winks and says, "Don't forget the shim sham shimmy lesson tomorrow night at the Clarendon Ballroom." As I head out, slowly past the "OPCORN" sign and back toward the parking lot, a smile emerges between my flushed cheeks, because traveling solo reminds me that I am in charge of my own good times and that, except when jiving, I do not need to link elbows with a man to feel complete.

GETTING BURIED ALIVE
2007

I can practically bring myself to tears with morbid fantasies. When a TV commercial aired for a movie about someone getting buried alive, I immediately pictured myself meeting such a fate. I tried to reason that of all the people I had ever known, and all the people each of them had ever known, I had never heard of anyone getting buried alive. The odds were against it. I mentioned this fright of going to my grave with a heartbeat to my friend Sally who told me Victorians were often buried with a cord in hand that was attached to a bell above ground, so the person could ring in the event of an error. A doorbell in reverse.

It's not that I am devoid of positive fantasies. I sometimes imagine meeting Mr. Right and living blissfully into old age. Somehow, though, getting buried alive seems more likely.

Two Sundays
2008

I am going to Paris to bicycle. No gazing at Cézannes, no browsing for the latest in footwear, no lingering over Bordeaux and smelly cheeses. Rolling along aimlessly, getting lost, not knowing what will happen next, and then writing about it, that is my plan. The egocentric thought occurs to me that I may be the only person in the history of the world to visit the City of Lights solely to cycle.

I have credentials: I've traveled to Paris several times, studied French in school and pedaled through the countryside of France as well as up hills in Tuscany, alongside the Danube in three different countries and throughout New York City's five boroughs. I've also clocked hundreds of miles wheeling all over Beijing, a challenge that ought to qualify me to bike on the moon. In Washington D.C., where I live, I ride my rusty 21-speed to dinner dates, baseball games, and shiva calls.

Vélib', the Paris public bicycle system, will allow me to

pick up a bike at any of the roughly fifteen hundred docking stations and drop it off at any station.

Ever since I first heard about this way of getting around the French capital, I have dreamed of trying it.

Back when I was between husbands and an optimistic twenty-something, I would arrive in a city without reservations and head to the most bustling part of town. Now, I spend hours in my kitchen searching the Internet for a hotel in Paris that seems most like home: away from the hubbub, on a residential street, with a garden perhaps. Although I have not completely shed my attraction to adventure, the years have added layers of anxiety. For my Paris bike trip, I load up with safety accoutrements: a whistle, a mirror with a strap to Velcro around a handlebar, and a reflective vest with two rows of blinking lights sewn into it. While packing my new green rain jacket and pants with welded seams, I daydream I'll be a trendsetter, wheeling beside the Seine in my other new garment, a tissue-thin, astronaut-worthy, neon yellow windbreaker.

Don't mistake me for a sleek, zippy cyclist hunched over racing-style handlebars. I am none of that. I plod along high and upright, arms spread wide, more Mary Poppins than Lance Armstrong. Seeking further promise that Parisian drivers will avoid hitting me, I affix a pair of large reflective dot stickers to both the front and back of my helmet, with the effect that when I wear it, my head takes on the appearance from any angle of a bulbous, yellow-eyed bug.

Additional unsettledness stems from too much ruminating about not being the center of anyone's life, which sometimes makes me feel envious of others' togetherness. It's a typical case of wanting what I don't have, not unlike the way I felt one evening while still married, lying on the floor beside

Jeff as we did our before-bed sit-ups. We were watching a TV profile of the aging Katherine Hepburn, a shot of her solitary figure on a sand dune, leaning back on her palms, legs outstretched, aristocratic chin tilted skyward. It made me wish I were unencumbered like that, the way I am now, which sometimes overwhelms me with a wave of isolation that sends me racing to hug my dog.

I worry about feeling lonely in Paris but, although I know a person or two there, I determine to pursue this cycling enterprise solo. Prone to turning my handlebars abruptly to admire a window box brimming with geraniums, I do not want to risk a biking buddy bumping into me. Being on my own offers the additional advantage that I won't have to pedal faster or slower to keep pace with someone or deal with another person's pangs of hunger or whims to shop. Yet I wish I could feel as ebullient about traveling singly as I did during my frolicsome twenties or as free as William Hazlitt does in his essay "On Going a Journey": "The soul of a journey is liberty, perfect liberty, to think, feel, do, just as one pleases." The conundrum—solitary freedom versus companionship at the cost of elbowroom—bedevils me.

I give more thought to how I will look while biking in Paris than I care to admit. Were I to exchange my "mom jeans," T-shirt, and sporty vest for the neck-swathed-in-scarf-sleek-boots look, I would fail to get it right. That does not restrain me from Googling "Paris style" while waiting for my morning tea water to boil, just to get a wee peek and maybe pick up a snappy accessory idea. I take it as a sign to embrace my fashion-challenged self when the first website listed bears the headline "Paris Style, Your Guide to Paris Hilton's Clothes." In fact, each time I search for something new about Paris the city, it is hard to avoid learning something new about Paris Hilton.

On the Sunday I arrive, I walk with trepidation through the early morning chill from my train stop to Hotel Millisime. I am not one of those who subscribe to the notion that "Oh, the hotel doesn't matter because you're hardly in the room." Even if I go to my room only to sleep, I carry with me the gestalt of its charm (or dreariness) throughout the day. Of course, one has one's own accommodation ideal. For me it's a multi-windowed modest-sized, carpeted room with white or pastel-painted furnishings and no dark wood in a quiet boutique hotel, the lobby of which eschews all hint of marble and gilt.

My fourth-floor quarters feature windows as big as doors that open to views of rooftops and chimneys on the row of white houses across the narrow Rue Jacob, which redeem the room's shortcoming of excessive beige. I drop my bags and set out to accomplish the modest goal of finding and biking the road along the Seine that is closed to traffic on Sundays. After walking two short blocks, I turn a corner and before me stand twenty of this city's twenty thousand sturdy, industrial gray bicycles, pleasingly parallel to one another.

Confronting my first Vélib' screen, I select the British flag option for instructions in English. After rejecting two credit cards, the machine accepts my American Express card, charging five euros for a one-week subscription. It spits out a ticket with my identification number, which I commit to memory. For each half hour of continuous use beyond the first thirty minutes, which are free, I'll be charged increasing amounts. My plan is to ride at little or no cost in thirty- or sixty-minute increments. If only computer dating were this user-friendly.

After sliding bike number eighteen from its post, I mount it and ride a few feet before getting off to adjust the saddle height, an operation I repeat two more times till I get it right. I then dismount again to measure the seat's stem—two hand widths minus one thumb—so I can make adjustments to future bike seats in advance of riding.

Despite proclamations that I'd pedal aimlessly, I had asked around and scoured websites for ideas. Alex, the French guy who cuts my hair, told me about a path along the Marne River, beyond the Bois de Vincennes, but it seems ambitious, even unsafe, to travel that far in my state of jet lag. I've also heard that several roads are closed to traffic on Sundays for the benefit of cyclists, rollerbladers, and those who just want to stroll. I decide to track down these traffic-free thoroughfares.

But first I must satisfy my curiosity about Hôtel des Grandes Écoles; if I like it, maybe I can move there. The hotel's website refers to it as "a pastoral cottage" with photographs to support the claim. They have been fully booked and have responded with polite no's to my daily e-mail inquiries about whether they've had a cancellation, yet my optimism is relentless in matters of lodging.

Four times during the short ride I pause to consult my map. Then, only blocks from the Seine, I come upon what looks like a French country house set back from the street. Smack in the middle of Paris, where space is scarce, a dazzling array of flowers rings the rich green lawn of the hotel's garden, which is the size of a petite park. To make matters worse, everyone who works here is so agreeable. A housekeeper is delighted to show me an assortment of rooms, all of which expose suitcases or other evidence of occupants.

I sit at a table on the patio beside a rainbow of posies and order a glass of grapefruit juice. Slouching down and resting my head on the white wrought iron chair back, I close my eyes and ask myself what I am doing here in this lovely garden, when frankly my garden at home is even lovelier with the added feature of my beagle boy's company. I try to shake the "shoulds" out of my mind, ones like *Is this quiet reclining really what I should be doing, given the time, anxiety and expense I invested to be in Paris?*

I swallow the last of my juice and then ask inside if perchance a cancellation has occurred in the past hour, since the last time I asked. No luck. As I walk to the nearby bike station, I make the case to myself that the rooms had peeling wallpaper, a weak argument, since I am attracted to a shabby chic look.

Pedaling in the street, I need to give full attention to staying alive. It has taken until mid-afternoon to simply arrive at a smooth path for cycling that allows me, for the first time, to notice my surroundings. All around, duos and trios of Parisians are talking, smiling, laughing. The city's entire population, it seems, is joyfully mingling on this blue-sky day, highlighting my solitariness; strangers' good times stand out in bold relief when I am on vacation and my own stakes to enjoy are high. Earlier, I had made a mental note to notice the ironwork on buildings, but all I see is the foreground, where everyone is having more fun than I am.

On the way back to my hotel, I spot a stream of cyclists alongside the Seine, and a young woman directs me to a ramp that leads down there. Finally I hit my stride, breezing along with the crowd, while a barge gliding in the opposite direction cuts a lazy swath in the gleaming water. Buildings across the river glow orange in the late afternoon sun. Even a flock of pigeons fluttering overhead provide a welcome sight. Soon, a police van comes into view and behind it cars, waiting, like a row of linebackers ready to pounce; the road is about to reopen to motor traffic.

The sheer pleasure of the past ten minutes has lifted me from my solitudinous freefall. I have locked in the memory of a perfect ride, never mind that it was only one-sixth of an hour. (It recalls a diet tip I once heard: when eating ribs do so in moderation because, regardless of whether you eat two or ten, you will remember that you ate ribs, not how many.) It also cheers me that tomorrow is Monday and Parisians will be back in their office cubicles rather than outdoors, flaunting their gaiety.

The next day, after a leisurely croissant and coffee, I see a guy at the Vélib' station kick tires and squeeze brakes before selecting his bike. So I kick and squeeze too. Then I pedal across the Seine on Pont Neuf alongside other cyclists: men in suits, women in high heels and a fellow chomping on a long baguette. Vélib' accounts for three of the five two-wheelers stopped beside me at a red light. My confidence must show because, as I weave through narrow lanes of the Marais, people stop me to ask directions.

During the days that follow, I explore other neighborhoods, getting lost in webs of one-way streets. Unlike in D.C. and Manhattan, no one yells at me when I ride on the sidewalk. I buy a compass on a cord that I can wear around my neck but can't figure out how it works, so I orient myself by asking a pair of fellows in T-shirts, *"J'ai une question stupide: Ou est La Seine?"* They point and then show me how the little green needle tip on my compass always faces north.

Each time I return a bike, I quiz other Vélib' users. I learn that riders turn the seat to face backwards when a bike need repair. One fellow tells me with glee that he no longer needs to take up space in his tiny apartment with a bicycle of his own. Another informs me that at first Parisians didn't like the Vélib' system; but then during a Metro strike, some commuters defied the law and wrapped locks around bikes at night to assure themselves rides in the morning. Everyone began using Vélib'. Well, not everyone. A student says he has friends who joined a Facebook hate group called "Anti Vélib.'"

If you ask what I favor about Vélib', it is the option of one-way trips, whereby I can cycle to dinner and then decide to take the Metro home. However, one night on the way back to my hotel, I would not have wanted to miss biking through a courtyard of the Louvre where I could peer at Venus de Milo (or an armless look-alike) through the museum's lit window. That was the evening I returned to my usual docking station and discovered all parking spaces taken, which led me to wonder how the very last person in Paris to return a bike on a given day manages, especially if the Vélib' screen shows the nearest available post to be on the opposite side of the city.

On a Saturday night, nearly a week after I arrived, a biking couple blows past me as though they are riding in a video game. Another couple pedals dreamily, holding hands. Without a soupçon of envy, I smile.

The end of a satisfying vacation is how I imagine the end of a life well-lived: you can relax because you know things turned out okay and you know where the good restaurants are. On my last day in Paris—a Sunday with the sky as parrot-blue as on that first, anxiety-ridden Sunday—I head to the river. Cruising the road along the Seine that is closed to traffic, the one that nearly eluded me a week ago, I roll past a photographer and his entourage, who are buzzing around a model wearing a strapless, emerald green ball gown. A little farther on, a few craggy men banter as they dangle fishing rods, and beside them an artist seated on a low stool dabs paint on a canvas. A couple, leaning on a bridge overhead, is sharing a pastry.

Near the Bastille, I admire swirls of ironwork on building facades. I chance upon a blocks-long market and, rather than return my bike while I browse, I use its attached lock to secure it to a post. For safekeeping, I deposit the key under a tissue in my cleavage. While inhaling the smell of ripe cheeses, I buy olives the color of spring grass and a slab of pink ham with a wide border of tantalizing fat. Within minutes of settling on a bench to eat, I am graced with hundreds of skaters rolling past me on their weekly police-escorted spin around the city.

Later, marionette music—not quite accordion, not quite calliope—attracts me with its Sunday-in-a-French-park sound. In fact, if I were composing a soundtrack for today, this would be it. Unquestionably, Loneliness will appear again to waggle its tongue at me, just as I can count on Euphoria to show up, sling an arm around my shoulder and skip me back to Paris, where I hear in winter you can ice skate aloft the Eiffel Tower. Although Paris has always been a romantic destination, I like knowing I can navigate it on my own.

THE LAST TIME I SAW PETER
WAS IN PARIS
2008

When he answers his phone, Peter's German-accented English sounds so familiar. "Of course I remember you. You had very long legs and a very short skirt."

I look down at my legs, now spotty with sun damage, and tell him, "I'm coming to Paris and thought we might meet for coffee."

"Ach, coffee. We have to have more than coffee." That's what I hoped he'd say.

The last time I saw Hilmar Peter was in Paris forty-two years ago, during my free-wheeling first trip to Europe. This time I am headed there to write a story about wheeling around on the public bicycle system. But having tracked down Peter, I am more inspired by the story that might unfold when he and I get together.

I wonder what he'll think of me, compared to the footloose twenty-year-old I had been. Back then I would show up in a city and rejoice in having no idea where I'd be sleeping that

257

night. And if my five dollars a day ran low, I thought nothing of making a meal from partially eaten sandwiches left behind on cafe tables. These days when I travel, I have rules. I require a confirmed room that has no big patterns on the wallpaper. And I carry a food bag from home that includes five varieties of pretzels.

Peter has rules too. He goes on to say he eats twice a day: breakfast at noon and ribs at three o'clock at his favorite Chinese restaurant. Suddenly, anyone eating three squares a day seems dull. Still, having to go for Chinese food in Paris?

We agree to meet at my Left Bank hotel, and I ask for his cell phone number. With the bachelor bravado of Henry Higgins, he replies, "I have no portable phone, no e-mail, no cat, no wife; I'm a happy man." By contrast, I have three phones, two e-mail addresses, one dog and two ex-husbands. Like Peter, I am happy, but I've been pondering for years how I might recapture the spirited girl I had been. I miss her.

What Peter does have, he says, is a spare bedroom I'd be welcome to use. On the flight to Paris, my mind sprints through ways this could play out. My right brain chirps, "Ooh, an exciting new romance possibility." My left brain cuts in, "Um, pining for a guy who brews his morning coffee (at noon) an ocean away? I don't think so."

"We'll see," I tell both my brains, secretly rooting for my right brain. When Peter and I first met, I had no left brain, only a right one that could fall in love with a distant stranger before he even came into focus.

On the day of our three o'clock meeting, after hours of pedaling along the Seine, I park my bike at two fifty-eight. As I race to meet Peter, I poof up my helmet hair with splayed fingers. Leaving no time to gussy up and change out of my neon yellow windbreaker is my left brain's idea, the notion that this rendezvous is out of mere curiosity.

Well, I soon regret the Lance Armstrong look because, at the hotel entrance, a silver-haired, movie-star-handsome man in blue jeans stands waiting in a Superman pose. He's still slender and looks remarkably fit, given his diet. Breathless, more from his gorgeousness than from rushing, I exhale, "Peter!"

"No," he answers, flashing a pity look with his Paul Newman eyes.

A few minutes later a paunchy, older fellow wearing chinos and walking shoes arrives. Can this be Peter, the same guy that rescued me in 1966 with a karate kick to the back of a Scottish wrestler who had me in his beefy grip?

"You look good," he says. He still has all his hair, no longer a mess of brown, but a gray crew cut.

"You're looking, um, fine yourself," I say.

We set off and as we stroll past patisseries and flower shops, Peter tells me that both of his parents lived to be one hundred and that in the late sixties he adopted a four-year-old girl in Africa, where he had been working. He shows me the scar on his wrist from a ritual blood exchange with her mother. The more outlandish his story, the more attractive he becomes.

He pauses in front of a bar called Miramar and says, "This is where you and I first met."

I press my face to the glass and see the narrow stairs I wandered down more than four decades ago into a smoky jazz cave. Across the cramped room a cute, skinny guy sat strumming guitar on a small stage. That summer I was traveling with a harmonica in my pocket, so I made my way over to him and asked, "*Jouez-vous* 'Swanee River?'" the only song I knew how to play other than "Moon River."

Peter and I performed a duet and from then on he called me Swanee. Later that night, we went for onion soup at Les Halles and paused on Pont Neuf to see who could spit farther into the Seine. By daybreak I had taken up residence with him at the top of countless stairs in his bathroom-sized flat—that had no bathroom—where the ceiling slanted over his sliver of a cot.

I was a free spirit only as long as I could sleep in my London Fog trench coat belted at the waist and as long as my Jewish parents, who lived a six-hour time difference away, did not know I was shacking up. With a German, no less. They disapproved of all things produced along the Rhine, and back then they were the ones with rules. This lent a Romeo-Juliet thrill to my romance with Peter, yet wherever we went, I was prepared to duck in case someone who knew my parents was passing by.

After nearly two weeks of tagging along on Peter's job, leading German tourists around Paris, my days felt too predictable. I became hungry for new possibilities, the surprise of what might happen next. There were other countries to see, other boys to meet. So, with a flourish of my Eurailpass, I waved auf Wiedersehen to Peter and boarded a train to Florence.

Now, forty-two years later, Peter and I enter his daily Chinese restaurant, which looks and smells like nearly every Chinese restaurant I have ever been to, dashing my hope that it would exude a French flair. When we sit down, Peter tells me he once worked with chickens and, therefore, does not like eating them. Then he orders chicken.

"Ribs are too messy to eat in front of a woman, with spitting out the bones," he says. He suggests I order my own dish, for which I am thankful, since sharing would require me to explain my objection to double dipping.

I ask what it was like growing up in Germany. He tells me that his father, an officer in the German army, had been away until 1943, the year Peter turned four. Upon returning from war, his father—still in uniform—offered young Peter a piece of candy. "I hesitated to take it, because he seemed like a stranger. Then, just as I reached for it, he pulled it back and put it into his own mouth. He was laughing. I never spoke to him again unless I had to."

While I am reeling from his father's sadistic prank and from Peter's capacity to hold a grudge, Peter reaches inside his tan leather zip-up jacket and withdraws a black notebook. He opens to a page filled with his original poems meticulously written in Japanese. "When I'm on the Metro," he tells me, "I translate them into French and German." How pleased I am to be sitting with Peter rather than with Superman of the Paul Newman eyes. Eccentric men like Peter make lousy boy-friends, but they captivate me because they are never boring.

For his next show and tell, Peter hands me a small photo album. As I flip through it, he provides commentary. My eyes become riveted to an old black and white shot of him, shirt-less. I begin to notice how quiet he's become. I look up to see him squeezing his head between his fists, like a vise. And I'm thinking, What is this?

"I swallowed a chicken bone," he gurgles.

"Oh, God!" I cry. "Do you want me to do the Heimlich?"

"No!" he answers, making more throat noises and point-ing to the photograph. "That picture was taken in Africa the year I adopted Rose."

"Oh, nice, really nice," I say, trying to act normal.

"And this one is Rose with her three children." He reaches

behind his head and pounds his back with his fist.

"Cute. So cute. Just adorable," I say and would have gone on this way, except that he bolts up, throws a fistful of euros on the table and announces, "I'm going to the hospital."

"Wait! I'll go with you."

"No! I want to go alone!"

As he dashes toward the door, I call after him, "Well phone, and let me know how you're doing."

The rest of the day, I alternate between worrying about him and thinking how embarrassed I'd be if I had choked on a chicken bone an hour into our reunion. I keep checking my cell. No messages.

Wait a minute, I wonder, did Peter fake the chicken bone as an exit strategy? Nah, my ego won't hear of it.

Before going to sleep, I phone him. No answer. I picture poor Peter lying in a cold hospital bed, or worse, on a cold stone slab, though I admit—due to my attraction to a good story—the idea of him dying from a chicken bone kind of appeals to me. But no, I really want to see him again and also hear more of his yarns. I drift off imagining Peter recovering and me moving to Paris.

I keep phoning. Two days after the fateful Chinese meal, I dial his number the second I wake up. You cannot imagine how relieved I am to hear his voice.

"Peter! You're alive!"

"No, this is Fredrik. No one has seen Peter for two days."

"Oh my God!" I say and explain about the chicken bone to Fredrik, a starving artist friend Peter had told me about. I ask him to call me if he hears any news.

All day I keep shaking my head, thinking, this can't really be happening.

That evening, my hands tremble as I dial again. Again a man answers. "Fredrik?"

"No, it's Peter."

"Peter! What happened to you?"

"Well, the first hospital transferred me to a second hospital, which is the only one in the world with this special way of removing the chicken bone." Is he making this up?

"How come no one knew where you were?"

"I told the hospital I had no family and no friends, because it was embarrassing and I wasn't going to tell anyone. But you told Fredrik and now everyone in Germany knows and everyone in Paris knows." Then, without any transition, he asks whether I want to go with him to see a Japanese Noh drama.

And I say, "No-o-o."

I'd seen enough drama. Disappearing for nearly three days without calling? I wave a nostalgic farewell to my free spirit and settle in with the comfort of rules. My right brain never had a chance.

SEARCHING FOR SUSAN FISHMAN
2008

I'd had this notion that once my divorce papers received a judge's stamp of finality I would still call myself Susan Orlins, but I would go back to being Susan Fishman, the one that Will at my divorce party recalled as "exotic" in a tone suggesting she had been a brand name.

With scores of friends and a calendar filled with guys to date, the social life of Susan Fishman's twenties and early thirties was the core around which swirled everything else. She threw parties with themes like "come as you are" and winged off twice a year to ski in Aspen and then sun in Negril before returning to Washington, D.C. and the city college classroom where she taught math.

Now, as a born-again unmarried, I wanted to boost my self-image as a fun, carefree sort. I tried channeling the age-appropriate gadabout, Auntie Mame. Yet I could not avoid noticing that my calendar—dinner with Alice, swing dancing (alone), singles Shabbat—bore little resemblance to the one from my previous bachelorettehood. The memory of Susan Fishman's devil-may-care ways and smooth-skinned, long-, dark-haired allure continued to hold power over me.

I still skied, still stood nearly five foot five and my teeth were still straight, though my almond-shaped brown eyes now had permanent, puffy half-moons beneath them. Yes, there had been a few hard-earned, post-divorce romances with baggage-laden men, like one who—whenever he felt blue— ate a pinch of his father's ashes. But none offered more than a flicker of everlasting possibility.

Could I be the culprit, more after the idea of a live-in than the actuality of one, given that my own suitcase is packed with, among other things, my need to have plans and my reluctance to commit?

How different we are, she and I. She played Scrabble for fun; I make a recording of all ninety-six two-letter words as well as U-less Q words and vowel dumps, like qwerty and looie, to memorize during long walks. She could show up in a strange town and within hours be clinking wine glasses over a steak dinner with a guy she just met. And she twinkled with the confidence that she could head sans ticket to a sold-out performance and wind up sitting in fifth row center. I wear the worried brow of a mother of three, who stresses about crickets in the basement and who, in that same basement, in the event of a terrorist attack, stores radio, dog food, The Official Scrabble Word List, Cipro, as well as Terazol 3 in the event of yeast infection from the Cipro.

Susan Fishman embraced the reverse of our mother's mantras; enough was never enough, nothing in moderation. After returning home on a Sunday night from a weekend camping trip with her boyfriend Elliott, she pleaded, "Let's find a camp-ground tonight and sleep out again." She even had an indul-gence plan for tragedy, telling a friend, "If I contract leprosy or something else scary happens, I'll eat an entire rare roast beef, then swallow a bottle of sleeping pills." What she had in mind was a painless, full-bellied conclusion.

I have the same attraction to pleasure that Susan Fish-man had, though no longer the same capacity. After the di-vorce a yellow caution light imbedded itself in my left cerebral hemisphere, and my optimism that things always had a way of working out grew shaky. I pine for those serotonin surges from the thrills S.F. lined up for herself, like soaring in a glider or hitchhiking in Jamaica, but it is now impossible to unlearn where danger lurks.

Plus, her thrills are no longer my thrills. If that is so then why can't I just accept that my greatest contentment arrives as the afternoon light dims and I ease into a big, soft chair, my feet on an ottoman, a book on my lap, and Casey's head on my thigh? Ah, lovely.

Maybe I have more in common with Susan Fishman than I am letting on since, like her, I have concocted a life with no two days the same. When there is no man in my life, I say to myself it would get boring to have someone around with re-quirements day after day to eat at a designated time. (I'm sure I would whistle a different melody if, in this bear market of men, I were to meet an appealing guy within a reasonable ra-dius of my age who also found me appealing, even if he—like my father—demanded dinner on the table at six.)

Could Susan Fishman have imagined a life like mine that lacks the unrelenting attention of men? Those who do show interest, I pick apart.

It was hard not to pick on the first day of a bicycle trip in France, when everyone was passing around sunscreen. This previously attractive man said he didn't wear sunscreen. With the finality of a light bulb that blows with a pop and makes you jump, his vain choice of suntan over skin protection ended all possibility of romance.

Sometimes I wish I were not so standoffish about men, because despite all my bear market hoo-ha, I am nearly positive my aloofness stems from never wanting to want something and not get it. That said, I'm not sure I feel like taking on one additional guaranteed loss in my future unless, of course, I were to predecease this imagined bedfellow.

Dark thoughts like this are as much a part of me as my esophagus, so there's another trait I share with Susan Fishman. I'm afraid I have given you the impression she was not a worrywart. To the contrary, though most people would not have guessed it, she had a solid capacity for negative fantasies; whenever cross-country skiing solo in the wilderness, for instance, she whipped up a collection of confrontations with bears, wolves, coyotes, bobcats, and mountain lions.

I try to remember how Susan Fishman's relationships with men concluded, but my sorrow-avoidance mechanism kicks in. Similarly, of the period immediately after I separated from my children's father, the darkest of my life, my first image is not of my hollow, amputated self, but of the cozy quarters I shared with my daughters in our new fatherless home. While the upstairs was being painted, we occupied two rooms in our basement with beds, dressers, piano, TV, and electric fry pan. Meals were intimate affairs, intimate because our round table with a glass of daisies in the center was so small and our common loss so raw.

Now, it's just Casey and me at home. The serenity is ideal for my writing, which earns enough to feed the dog and pay for bicycle tune-ups. Because I divorced well, I don't need to scour help wanted ads. And there is the rub. I'm not complaining, but as a freelance writer, I have no anchor, no office culture. I regret that, as a competent loner, I have built more space around myself than I presently need. Luckily, I have amassed enough friends to form a small village. So there's always someone to bike to whenever I'm desperate to escape the racket of molecules banging together or whatever you want to call the sound of silence.

Maybe I could do more to attract the company of a man. Instead, I have headed down a path of comfort in mom jeans. By contrast, some women I know have undergone the cosmetic blade to look sexier and younger. Would I ever pay a surgeon to cut open my face and staple my head? Certainly not to attract a guy who won't wear sunscreen. Maybe, rather than searching for Susan Fishman, it would be a better idea to search for Susan Orlins.

How did I go from being Susan Fishman to being Susan Orlins? There came a time when Susan Fishman slipped away and then returned in sensible shoes as the Susan Fishman of mothers, romancing her children with relentless gratification. In countless coffee shops, mother Susan Orlins hung toddler Eliza from a Sassy Seat and they chattered about the day, while Jeff roamed China on business trips.

Now that my girls are in their twenties, I envy their lives. But it is the me I am now who appreciates the texture and richness of their adventures, which are somewhat opposite from what Susan Fishman strove for. I doubt she would have traded her summers of driving around the country and hanging out at tennis tournaments in order to pursue—as my girls have—defending the poor in New York City, studying in China, or leading students on wilderness adventures with the weight of a forty-pound pack on her hips. Although I would not trade a minute of my youth (would I?), I ache with the joy I envision if I had lived my children's lives, except for all the homework. It's a moot point, of course, but I want both what they have and what I had.

This envy of my children's world is different from my wistful dwelling on Susan Fishman's life. For one thing, there is the obvious motherly fulfillment of seeing one's offspring take flight so merrily, not to mention what I skim from their exploits to savor vicariously for myself. Sometimes, though, I worry I'll turn into my Aunt Lolly, who paid monthly visits to each of her grown daughters around the country, and then returned to her own home to plan her next round of visits.

Susan Fishman and I—the me before I married my children's father for eighteen years, and the me I am now—are like strangers who sit in close proximity on a train but never meet, each musing to ourselves about the other, *She seems nice.* I ruminate how, well, exotic it would be if I could dust off the years and sun damage and unearth Susan Fishman. Would she be who I think she was? Would I want to be her?

I picture myself on a sunny Saturday afternoon walking up the path to her Georgetown apartment, my stomach churning, as though she were a child I had given up for adoption and we were about to come face-to-face for the first time in decades. I ring the bell, then smooth out my skirt while I wait for her to open the door. Her hair falls in a low, loose ponytail nearly to her waist. She is wearing a mini dress that looks like an elongated tie-dyed T-shirt, revealing long, slender, suntanned legs. For a moment, I feel even more self-conscious than usual about the sun spots on my own legs. Then her smile lassoes me in.

"Hi," she says in that tone that got her elected friendliest girl in ninth grade.

"I am so excited to see you," I say in that tone that got me elected friendliest girl in ninth grade. I hug her and say, "I can't believe I'm actually meeting you."

"Come in," she says and gestures for me to sit on the sofa, an assemblage of cinderblocks, a door, and a mattress. Deviled eggs, steak tartare, and a bottle of Gallo Hearty Burgundy await us by the window on a wooden table I know to be wobbly.

As usual under pressure, all thoughts have evacuated my mind, so I ask, "How are you?"

"Great," she answers, while unscrewing the wine cap.

Wanting to test the accuracy of my memory, I say, "So, tell me about your life and whether you're happy." I am too impatient to ask only one question at a time.

"On my days off from teaching, I get out of bed and dream up what I want to do. If it's nice out, I might bike to the river with my paints or go to the courts and watch a trial. I carry a bag of popcorn in my bicycle basket in case I decide to go to an afternoon movie. On Sundays, I sell my paintings at the flea market. Selling is my favorite part of painting. Sometimes I think I paint just so I'll have something to sell."

She laughs, her *joie de vivre* palpable. It surprises me that she does not mention romance; is it conceivable I've fabricated that boyfriends loomed so large in her mind?

She offers me a blob of steak tartare on a slice of cocktail rye and says, "Remember how Mom used to pop a handful of

raw meat into our mouths when she was making hamburgers?" as if we had shared a childhood as sisters.

"I'm only having this because today's a special occasion,"
I tell her and bite into it. "I still love raw meat, but I don't risk
eating it anymore."

The tartare highlights one of our painful differences. My
risk aversion causes me to miss out, while being gung ho to
try everything is part of her carefree Peter Pan.

"I think this cautiousness started to get out of hand after I had kids," I say, and then I jump from risk to a sunnier
topic. "I wish you could meet my daughters. They would love
you and you would adore them." She herself seems like an es-
tranged daughter, and I feel hopelessly frustrated that we can't
always be together.

"I guess I'll get to meet them eventually," she quips.

I want her to admire me, so I tell her I still hope to live
out our fantasy of donning a high hat and becoming a horse
and buggy driver. I omit that after meeting a man who owned
some carriages, I passed up the opportunity to work for him
when I became besieged by images of out-of-control horses
on the Capitol steps with me at the reins.

"Can you imagine ever being like me?" I ask. "Someone
who wants to be easygoing like you, but who overthinks every
move?"

A smile spreads across her face and then her brow fur-
rows. She says it may not show but she has a lot of fears, of
things like fires and robbers. Then she asks me what I know to
be her most nagging concern. "What was it like to be with the
same man for so many years?"

I tell her that he and I were a good match and that he never got in the way of my independence. But this isn't what she's

after, so I add that even sex with the same man for all those years, though not holding surprises and dwindling in frequency, was   surprisingly satisfying and that the passion I missed from not having one new relationship after another appeared in boundless measure for my kids. That never fades.

I don't want to spoil the surprise of her future by revealing too much about the global adventures I shared with Jeff. It occurs to me she would not be terribly impressed anyway, given her incuriosity about the world.

The sudden reminder of her pinhole lens—how little interest she has in pursuits that have meant so much to me—makes me startle and want to go charge my brain with a book. This fissure in her razzle-dazzle sparks in me a renewed appreciation for Susan Orlins and recalls a recent evening when I described Susan Fishman to a friend. "She sounds like a ditz," he said. "I'm glad I know you instead of her."

She doesn't seem to notice the gulf between us that I'm now feeling. We continue to eat and laugh about shared experiences, such as the tartare-off party she threw, where guests voted her raw meat creation tastiest of all the tartares brought by friends. Before I leave, she gives me a tour of her one-bedroom apartment and *I wonder to myself, I wonder what ever happened to this cute little wrought iron table beside her bed?*

Again, we hug at the door, and I tell her, "I wish you well." It's the kind of thing I say out of habit.

Postscript

WHAT IF I MEET A GUY I LIKE?
2012

Sometime during the decade of the 00s, I begin to worry, *What if I meet a guy I like?*

Monday: He gets up. I want to stay in bed but now I can't fall back to sleep. Or, I get up and he wants to sleep, so I can't turn on NPR.

Ah, breakfast! I make myself French toast and a cup of steaming black coffee, and just as I'm about to sit down and enjoy reading the *Times*, he trots in and says, "Mm, that smells good."

He never eats French toast or I would have made enough for him. I share mine because otherwise I'd feel guilty. But now I feel hungry and my peaceful breakfast with newspaper indulgence is spoiled.

I walk the dog after which I set up my laptop to work outdoors.

He asks if I want to bike along the river with him. I'm conflicted because a bike ride sounds great but so does my routine of working outdoors. Either way I'll be frustrated; I'll regret that I made the wrong choice.

The day rumbles along like this with either interruptions or too many choices. Lord knows there were enough choices before he came along. On the other hand, some of the choices I used to enjoy, like walking with friends, have been reduced because of the time I spend biking and hanging out with him.

Night draws nigh and with it comes the daily discussion of what, when, and where to eat. He feels like going out. I feel like eating at home. He's hungry now and wants real food; I'm not and I don't. I just polished off a chunk of dark chocolate, a handful of almonds, and a large glass of milk, which will keep me satisfied for hours (my favorite diet tip).

I long for the nights before he came along when the second I got hungry I could stand by the kitchen TV watching *The Bachelor*, while whumping down stuffed grape leaves and picking at prosciutto without soiling any plates or utensils.

We end up eating at home and, after dinner, he wants to settle in with cops and robbers or the local news on TV, but I don't like those scary shows. Casey, who used to rest his head on my lap, jumps onto his lap.

A while later, one of us is ready to go to bed; the other isn't. One of us wants to have sex; the other doesn't.

He raises the thermostat. After his breathing shifts into slumber, I lower the thermostat.

Tuesday to Friday: It's the same. (He is retired.) Except Wednesday nights I watch *Survivor* and he sulks.

Saturday and Sunday: When you don't go to an office

during the week, weekends aren't all that different, but after a lifetime of conditioning, they feel different. On Saturday night, he thinks we should go out to dinner and a movie. I get rattled by noisy eating establishments and crowded theaters. It's a perfect night to be cozy at home.

There must be reasons people pair off into living spaces, but I can't remember what those reasons are.

Of all the things I worry about, finding a mate is not one of them unless you count the worry that I *will* meet someone I like.

GUIDE FOR FURTHER DISCUSSION

1. Talk about your most memorable crush, the one you "never forgot."

2. Early in her marriage to Jeff, Susan moves their living quarters in the Peking Hotel from a bright room with a view on a high floor to a dark room facing a gray building on a lower floor. Jeff becomes angrier than she has ever seen him. She thinks it could mean divorce. Discuss how you resolve conflicts in your marriage or other relationships. How do you and your partner express anger? How do you react to each other's anger?

3. Discuss passion or lack thereof in marriages and/or long-term relationships. In what ways do you think couples can keep the romance and passion alive? How important are

romance and passion in a relationship? How important is sex as you grow older?

4. Susan explores how annoying she is to her children. How annoying are you to your kids or to your parents? How annoying are they to you? What can be done to reduce all the annoyingness?

5. Susan worries about her dog's self-esteem and whether or not he is bored. How do you enrich your pet's life? If you don't have a pet, discuss a childhood pet or the choice to be petless.

6. What is or was your relationship with your mother like? How did it change over time? If your mother died when you were young, how did you handle that? Did you have someone who became a surrogate mother? What advice would you give to a young person who loses a mother?

7. In what ways, if any, do you long for your younger self? In what ways are you glad to no longer be your younger self?

8. What does happiness mean to you? How has your definition of happiness changed over the years?

ACKNOWLEDGMENTS

Medical writer and author Joan Liebmann-Smith has read just about everything I've ever written. For years she edited with a sharp eye that taught me much of what I know. Her endless encouragement and friendship kept me going.

Author Richard Liebmann-Smith has read much of my writing. His eagerness to offer creative approaches as well as to harp on structure during late-night conversations have made me a better writer. His humor helped keep me sane.

Steve Wasserman's interest in my writing and his willingness to carve out time from his busy life to counsel me has meant so much.

Author, humorist and lost-then-found high school friend, Jon Winokur, a.k.a. Jonnie, came back into my life via Twitter. With tough, honest talk about what it takes to make a book succeed, he provided me with an invaluable perspective on publishing, alerting me to the worst possible outcome while encouraging me to reach for the best.

Designer Rodrigo Corral—with humor, concept, and sheer talent—captured me and my *mishegasses* so deftly for the cover of my book that friends and family upon seeing it said, "That's so you!"

Rachel Adams explained every detail of the cover design and understood my goals so well that she succeeded in assuaging my anxieties, allowing me to worry less and write more.

My writing group—Colleen Cordes, Chris Intagliata, Robyn Jackson, Mandy Katz, Sue Katz Miller, and Karen Paul-Stern—has elevated not only my writing but also my spirits ever since I had the good fortune to join. A diverse collection of talented authors, they critique with candor ("cringe-worthy") while providing endless encouragement ("Who should play you in the film version?" "I'll lend you my red dress for the red carpet.").

The most promising writer I know, Lily Lopate, never fails me with her candid critiques that raise my writing to a higher plane. In her own personal essays, she deepens the discourse by questioning herself from every angle, which helps remind me to do the same.

Anita Bernstein cannot imagine how much it meant to me that she read my entire manuscript . . . twice! She picked up on nuances that made a big difference in the final copy.

Endless thanks to Jane Bressler, who contributed picky edits and comments that made me laugh. Nothing escaped her sharp eye.

Brenda Barbour and I were a writing group of two. I would be ready to deep-six an essay, and she would point out what she liked about it. At once, I would see it as she did and revise the piece to one that made it into print. Those afternoons inspired me.

Whenever I am out of ideas, I meet Elissa Parker for a veggie wrap. After chatting with her for an hour, I bike home with a whole new list of worrisome things to write about. Her willingness to talk about every aspect of my book and reply to my late-night panicky e-mails has sustained me.

My life improved significantly after I met Kim Gledhill, who agreed to design the book's layout. How did I get so lucky?

Amber Keyser's patience and design skills helped me to worry less as I fussed over things like squiggles on italicized Ls.

My sincere gratitude to photographers Mark Fishman, Rob Black, Wayne St. John, Peter Nagy, Irv Nathanson, and Sue Lasky for their efforts to improve my image. It took a village....

How can I ever thank Scott Bressler, a genius, who responds to my pleas for tech help, any time of day or night, and who persists until he solves a problem, expecting nothing in return? Scott, you are my hero.

Eugene Keyzman similarly rescues me from tech Hell within moments no matter where in world my e-mails find him.

My assistant Tracy Gaudet lives a time zone away. We have never met in person, but she has miraculously expanded her day to help publish this book, awakening some days at the same hour I go to sleep, while her three small children are still deep in slumber. There is no chance this book would have come to fruition without her dedication, organization, and sheer brilliance.

When my children—Eliza, Sabrina, and Emily Orlins— like what I've written, I know I've done something right. They tweet and Facebook and tell their friends about my blog. I experience joy, unlike any other, whenever they or one of their friends compliments something I've produced. This book is dedicated to my three daughters, who make me smile every day, and to my parents—now deceased—whose laughter, wisdom, and faith in me I cherish.

I'm worried to death I have forgotten someone. I have so many dear, supportive friends that mean the world to me, including my committee (you know who you are), who patiently voted on things like cover design and photos as well as on whether I should worry that a line would offend Gentiles and whether a sex scene made me seem too slutty.

Finally, for their contributions to my ability to complete this book, I acknowledge my ADD coach, my personal organizers, and all but perhaps two or three of the psychotherapists I have known over the years. Although I have learned from all of my therapists, a special note of gratitude to my extraordinary cognitive therapist, who contributed in so many ways to the outcome of this book.

16816942R00176

Made in the USA
Charleston, SC
12 January 2013